Notorious Divorces

NOTORIOUS DIVORCES

by EDWARD Z. EPSTEIN

Lyle Stuart, Inc.   *Secaucus, N. J.*

First edition

Copyright © 1976 by Edward Z. Epstein

All rights reserved, including the right to reproduce
this book or any portion thereof in any form

Published by Lyle Stuart, Inc.
120 Enterprise Ave., Secaucus, N. J. 07094
Published simultaneously in Canada by George J. McLeod Limited
73 Bathurst St., Toronto, Ont.

Address queries regarding rights and permissions
to Lyle Stuart, Inc.

Manufactured in the United States of America

LIBRARY OF CONGRESS CATALOGING IN PUBLICATION DATA

Epstein, Edward Z
    Notorious divorces.

    1. Divorce—United States.   2. Divorce—United
States—Cases.   I. Title.
HQ834.E66   301.42′84′0973   76-40256
ISBN 0-8184-0224-5

Photographs: UPI and the New York *Daily News*

With a very special thank you
to Stephen G. Epstein

Contents

Introduction

Animosity. Revenge. Retribution. Bitterness.

All the things that make life worthwhile—if you're a divorce lawyer. The matrimonial battleground has been, and continues to be, the scene of some of the most colorful episodes in America's marital history: Exposés, confrontations, and revelations.

The war between husbands and wives is, of course, no laughing matter. A matrimonial contest often results in love turning to hate. "Vengeance!" becomes the order of the day. Formerly gentle spouses turn into seething monsters, lashing out and exposing family skeletons in order to "teach that son-of-a-bitch (husband/wife) a lesson." If one partner has become sexually enslaved by the other, the urge to destroy the wanderer becomes almost overwhelming.

In the fierce struggle to "win," children become pawns and reputations are ruined, all in the name of "doing the right thing." It's amazing how even the most celebrated and revered personages will behave irrationally when involved in a divorce action. Caution is thrown to the winds. Dirty linen is aired in public.

In the past ten years the divorce rate has nearly doubled, and in 1975 the number of marriages ended by divorce or annulment exceeded the million mark for the first time. It is almost impossible to believe that there was one divorce for every two marriages last year. "Irreconcilable Differences" is heard in the courts almost as frequently as "Guilty" or "Not Guilty," and it would seem that marriage vows should now include: "Until divorce do us part!"

Here are spectacular divorce cases that have captured the attention of the world. Much new information sheds interesting light on the persons involved: Rockefellers, Stillmans, Rhinelanders, Bronfmans, Barbara Hutton and her seven husbands, and Tommy Manville and his eleven wives.

Edgar M. Bronfman

versus

Lady Carolyn Bronfman

Is there sex after marriage?

Apparently for Edgar Bronfman, head of the largest liquor corporation in the world, the answer was a resounding *no!* For Bronfman and his bride, Lady Carolyn Townshend of England, their marriage was sex-on-the-rocks starting with the wedding night.

The honeymoon was no improvement.

No was the story of the entire eleven-month marriage between the head of Seagrams and Lady Carolyn But the answer had always been an equally resounding *yes!* before the wedding. Marriage can sometimes wreck a pleasant relationship.

The details of the romance and the eleven-month lack of wedded bliss were brought out in an annulment action finally instituted by Bronfman in the Supreme Court of the State of New York on the ground that the marriage had never been consummated. The trial was held before Justice Jacob Grumet, without a jury. It started on November 4, 1974.

Edgar Bronfman is president of Distillers Corporation–

9

Seagrams Ltd., the General Motors of the liquor industry. The company was brought to that position of eminence by his father, the legendary Samuel Bronfman, who entered the liquor business in 1915, selling by mail order in Canada. In 1924 the elder Bronfman and his brothers built their first small distillery in Montreal, and thereafter they established a business relationship with Joseph E. Seagram & Sons.

The small Bronfman company grew, and then Prohibition in the United States brought a business boom. The Bronfmans used a separate family-owned company, Atlas Shipping, as a go-between in Seagram liquor transactions with American bootleggers.

Atlas bought whiskey from Seagram or imported it from abroad and then resold it to American mobsters, who made hundreds of millions of dollars violating the Eighteenth Amendment, with the help of millions of otherwise law-abiding American citizens.

At first Atlas shipped much of its whiskey to Windsor, Ontario, where it was turned over to bootleggers, who loaded it onto speedboats for a quick trip across the mile-wide Detroit River. In 1930, however, the Canadian government, in an apparent effort to cooperate with the United States in its "noble experiment," blocked the export of liquor to any destination where its importation was prohibited.

When direct exports were banned, Atlas opened a branch office, the Northern Export Company, in Saint Pierre, the largest village in the French-owned Saint Pierre and Miquelon Island group, about fifteen miles off the Newfoundland coast.

Bronfman purchased whiskey from Seagram and other distillers and legally shipped it to the islands, which were French soil. The liquor was then sold to bootleggers, loaded on ships in the ice-free Saint Pierre harbor, and carried down east to "Rum Row," a line of mother vessels anchored outside the jurisdiction of the United States Coast Guard. In 1931 enough Canadian whiskey landed in Saint Pierre to provide every man, woman, and child in the island with thirty gallons a week.

Prohibition came to an end on December 5, 1933, and the records of the Atlas Shipping Company were destroyed at about the same time. No one really knew how much of that company's whiskey actually filtered into the United States during Prohibition. Samuel Bronfman said, "We loaded carloads of goods, got our cash, and shipped it. We shipped a lot. Of course, we knew where it went, but we had no legal proof. And I never went on the other side of the border to count the empty Seagram bottles." That was a good way of not knowing.

After Prohibition, by brilliant business maneuvering and with a good deal of business courage, the Bronfmans grew bigger and better. Their control of Distillers Corporation–Seagrams Ltd. made them a prime factor in the liquor business. In 1974 they were selling more than a hundred different brands in 119 countries, with sales of almost two billion dollars.

Bronfman investments, through CEMP (an acronym for Samuel Bronfman's children—Charles, Edgar, Minda, and Phyllis), a family holding corporation, branched out into other fields that included brewing, packaging, computer services, oil companies, and real estate.

The only business setback Edgar Bronfman ever had was his effort to gain a foothold in the motion picture industry by an attempt to acquire control of Metro-Goldwyn-Mayer. He finally lost out in his bid for control to Kirk Kerkorian, a Las Vegas casino operator, who had to put up more than one hundred million dollars to take the plum from Bronfman.

However, since Bronfman made an ultimate profit of more than fifteen million dollars on his investment, it can hardly be called an unsuccessful business venture. One can become rich with setbacks like that.

Today, Bronfman-controlled corporations are Canada's largest owners of real estate, including shopping centers, office buildings, hotels, and department stores. It is estimated that the Bronfman investment in these enterprises will total more than five hundred million dollars by 1978.

Among large real estate holdings in the United States is the monumental thirty-eight-story bronze Seagram Building in New York, which opened in December 1957. Considered one of the most beautiful office buildings in the country, it is also one of the most valuable.

In 1957, at twenty-eight, Edgar became President of Joseph E. Seagram & Sons, the United States subsidiary that accounted for 90 percent of the business of Distillers Corporation–Seagrams Ltd. Samuel Bronfman wanted Edgar to take over and run things so he could "make mistakes while my eyes are still open."

But Edgar did not make many mistakes, and he gradually acquired the experience the elder Bronfman apparently felt he needed. By 1962 Edgar was really running the company, and executives, many old enough to be his father, knew it. There was little doubt of his ability, and the respect in which he was held by his peers was not for Samuel Bronfman's son, but for Edgar in his own right.

As Edgar said, "I became president *de jure* in 1957 and *de facto* in 1962."

Edgar Bronfman was born in Canada in 1929, the third of four children including two older sisters and a younger brother. He attended elementary school in Montreal and preparatory school in Ontario. From there he went to Williams College in Massachusetts, where he played the role of a rich man's son, wrecking a succession of cars and motorcycles. After three years at Williams he came home to Montreal's McGill University, from which he graduated in 1951.

In 1953 Edgar married Ann Loeb, the daughter of John Loeb, then a senior partner in Loeb, Rhoades & Company, a prestigious Wall Street financial house. At the wedding Carl M. Loeb, grandfather of Ann and the multimillionaire founder of the company, impressed by the great wealth of the Bronfmans (which then exceeded four hundred million dollars), said, "At my age I am not sure I can adjust to the idea of being a poor relation."

Edgar and Ann Bronfman lived an unpublicized married life. They had five children and kept their private life private. In 1973 there was the first public inkling of irreconcilable differences.

They were divorced in that year.

Edgar Bronfman first met Lady Carolyn in London in 1968. She was the twenty-eight-year-old daughter of the seventh Marquis Townshend of Norfolk, England. They saw each other infrequently, and there was no hint of anything between them except a pleasant social relationship.

They renewed their acquaintance several years later when Carolyn began working in the public-relations department of the Seagrams New York office. By then the British socialite had been married and divorced from Antonio Capellini, who bore the title Patrician of Genoa, Italy.

In 1972 there was no public hint that the Bronfmans were anything but happily wed, but in fact they were heading for the marital rocks. At this time, as Bronfman later testified, "My marriage was about to dissolve." He poured his troubles into the willing and sympathetic ears of Carolyn, and in December 1972 a romance started between the Lady and the liquor tycoon.

During the annulment hearings details of the romance emerged. In 1973 Bronfman and the fair lady took trips abroad together. At one such sojourn in Paris, Bronfman discussed marriage to the willowy blonde, who was very receptive to the idea. However, she expressed fears about her financial security or, as she put it, "financial insecurity." Why she would have financial fears marrying Bronfman was a mystery.

To set her mind at ease about money, Bronfman agreed to give her four thousand dollars a month over and above household expenses once she became Mrs. Edgar M. Bronfman. That seemed to calm her, and they set a wedding date of December 18, 1973.

Apparently in anticipation of a happy married life, Bronfman made a magnanimous gesture in an antenuptial agreement. He gave the lady of his choice $1 million in cash, $115,000 worth of jewels, and the deed to his baronial estate in Yorktown Heights, one of the showplaces of Westchester County, New York.

This seemed to be the soul of generosity, and almost anyone would have been happily satisfied. But apparently not Lady Carolyn. She wanted more, more, more! The British socialite, quite obviously being egged on by someone, kept up her money demands. Bronfman later testified, "She suggested that her family had advised her that because I was a man of means, one million was a paltry sum and I should settle five million dollars on her." Five million!

When Justice Grumet asked, "What was your response?" Bronfman replied, "I did not respond." Which seemed very sensible.

The wedding took place at the St. Regis Hotel in New York on December 18, 1973, but nothing else did. His wife requested a surprised and shocked Bronfman to sleep at his Park Avenue apartment, while she stayed at the hotel. That was quite a night for Bronfman.

"Did you ask to have relations with Lady Carolyn?" asked Justice Grumet.

"I did, but I was turned down," Bronfman answered sadly. It was somewhat ego shattering to be "turned down" on one's wedding night, especially when one is rich, and handsome enough to have strangers wonder whether he is a movie star.

Later Carolyn testified it had been Bronfman's idea that he spend the wedding night alone in his apartment.

"You mean he volunteered to go home?" asked Justice Grumet.

"Absolutely!" answered Lady Carolyn.

"Now I've heard everything!" whispered an incredulous reporter to a fellow newsman.

Lady Carolyn insisted that Bronfman's departure from the St. Regis to his apartment stunned everyone. "I was distraught and in tears when he went to his house rather than spend the night with me."

However, although Bronfman may have spent his wedding night alone, Lady Carolyn apparently did not. A witness, Nels R. Johnson, a friend of Carolyn's, testified that Doctor Sheldon Glabman, a New York specialist in internal medicine, had told him that the bride had spent part of her wedding night with him.

On the witness stand a very agitated and flustered Dr. Glabman, subpoenaed by Bronfman, refused to answer questions on the subject. Bronfman's lawyer asked him, "Is it not a fact that, before she married Mr. Bronfman, Lady Carolyn and you were lovers?"

"I refuse to answer that on constitutional grounds," Glabman answered.

"Is it not a fact," the lawyer continued, "that the day before the marriage and the day after the marriage, she said to you that the ring that would go on her finger would be your ring and not his?"

"No," the doctor replied, almost shouting.

After consulting his lawyer, however, Glabman said that he had had a conversation with Lady Carolyn about a ring during March or April. But he again refused, on constitutional grounds, to reveal the substance of the conversation. Justice Grumet upheld Glabman's refusal to answer.

According to Bronfman, the honeymoon was no improvement over the wedding night.

For their honeymoon, the newlyweds flew to Acapulco in separate planes of the Seagrams air fleet. It was a startling honeymoon in more ways than one.

They were accompanied on the planes by his mother, her mother, their sons by former marriages, and Lady Carolyn's sister. To make certain the couple would not be lonesome with only relatives, a group of friends came along. "Now, that's a honeymoon!" quipped amazed observers.

Acapulco nights are conducive to romance, but the whispering breeze did nothing to affect Lady Carolyn's sleeping habits. As far as Bronfman was concerned, it was more of the same. The answer was *no*, and so it continued. During the honeymoon Bronfman would find sex only by looking it up in the dictionary.

Carolyn testified that nothing happened the first few nights of their honeymoon because Bronfman was "unromantic."

"I told Edgar he had not been very affectionate with me," she said. "He put his hand on mine and said, 'I'm horny.' I said, 'How can you say anything like that to me? That's not very romantic.'"

In a soft, almost inaudible voice she claimed, however, that the marriage was consummated later during the honeymoon.

This was met by a complete and emphatic denial by Bronfman.

They returned to New York from the "honeymoon," again in separate planes, and started living apart—she at the St. Regis, he at his Park Avenue apartment. For Bronfman, his new marriage was a romantic nightmare.

In her testimony, Lady Carolyn conceded that she had not had sexual relations with Bronfman on their wedding night because "it wasn't the right time of the month." But from the testimony of Bronfman, apparently there *was* no right time of the month. As someone remarked, as far as Lady Carolyn was concerned Bronfman could look forward to sex on the thirty-second day of each month.

Carolyn said she was "ready, willing, and able" to be a wife. According to Bronfman she was able, but not ready or willing. Obviously, for Bronfman, marriage to Carolyn was not the way to get her to go to bed.

Lady Carolyn "had a hangup about sex after the marriage and she would not sleep with me," said Bronfman. He further said that this was difficult to understand, since he and Carolyn had no hangup or difficulty in having sexual relations before the wedding.

When Carolyn's lawyer asked him how many times they had had sexual intercourse before their marriage, Bronfman at first answered that he could not remember.

"Was it at least ten times?" asked the attorney.

"More. I really didn't keep count," Bronfman replied.

"Was it more than twenty-five times?"

"Yes!" Bronfman responded emphatically.

Bronfman may have found it difficult to find an explanation for Lady Carolyn's postmarriage actions, but a witness, Nels R. Johnson, believed he had the answer.

Johnson, who had previously described himself as a long-time friend of the titled Englishwoman, testified that he had discussed the case with Carolyn in Switzerland "two months ago."

Recalling the conversation Johnson said, "She told me Edgar had screwed a lot of people and 'it gives me a lot of satisfaction to screw him without having to deliver.' "

Feeling that Johnson had put too much emphasis on the word *screw* and was using it for shock effect, Lady Carolyn's lawyer asked the witness, "How many times did she use the word *screw* in that conversation?"

Unperturbed, the witness said with a smile, "I don't remember."

The only unanswered question was *why* Lady Carolyn was acting in this surprising manner to one who was so generous to her and could have been even more generous in the future.

Again a possible answer was supplied by Johnson. Apparently, Carolyn was infatuated with Doctor Glabman. Johnson testified, "Glabman told me that the doctor-patient relationship had blossomed into a love affair," and the titled English beauty "pursued him like no man had ever been pursued," showering him with thousands of dollars' worth of gifts. It seemed that Carolyn's thoughts about sex were on the doctor and not on Bronfman.

In an effort to destroy Johnson's credibility, Carolyn's lawyer tried to show that he was a cast-off lover of the lady and that this was his way of getting back at her.

"Were you ever in love with Lady Carolyn?"

"Yes, for a short time."

"Are you not a spurned lover of Lady Carolyn?"

Johnson, an elegantly tailored man in his thirties, reflected for a moment and answered, "I hardly think that is true. My answer is no."

Lady Carolyn denied that she had become Glabman's lover. However, under cross-examination she admitted having been intimate with the doctor at the Stanhope Hotel in New York. In fact, she said, "Doctor Glabman moved into the hotel and took a room next to mine."

Justice Grumet asked the English socialite directly whether she had sexual intercourse with Glabman.

"Eventually, yes," answered Carolyn.

The judge said he did not understand what this answer meant, and Lady Carolyn said, "Yes, I had." That answer was easily understood.

Edgar M. Bronfman was granted an annulment.

Justice Grumet said the annulment was justified because Lady Carolyn had "induced Mr. Bronfman into marriage by promising to live with him as a dutiful and loyal wife," but in reality, testimony during the two-week trial showed that the marriage had not been consummated.

In an order signed December 16, 1974, it was adjudged and decreed that the marriage was null and void and that Lady Carolyn was to redeliver to Bronfman the deed to the estate in Yorktown Heights.

It was further ordered that Carolyn was to return the one million dollars Bronfman had given her, that the antenuptial agreement was null and void, and that she would "immediately and forever refrain from using the surname *Bronfman* in identifying herself."

Whether Justice Grumet would have awarded Lady

Carolyn any compensation for her unwifely activities is pure speculation. However, the attorneys for both parties (with Bronfman's consent, of course) agreed that he would pay Carolyn forty thousand dollars per year for eleven years ". . . in full settlement of all her present and future claims against the plaintiff."

It would seem that Edgar Bronfman received very little for the $440,000, even allowing for inflation.

James A. Stillman

versus

Anne U. Stillman

The weather, quite cool for a June morning, turned pleasantly warm toward noon as a shining bride emerged from a carriage drawn by two prancing horses. She smiled happily at a large group in front of the magnificent church, and the crowd, having impatiently waited an hour for a glimpse of the well-publicized beauty, burst into applause and shouted good wishes.

The bride, Anne Urquhart Potter, basked in the adulation. She was about to be married to handsome banking heir James Stillman, Jr., in Grace Church, in New York. It was June 3, 1901. This was the social event of the season, with most of the big names of the Four Hundred in attendance.

The trip to the altar had not been an easy road for Anne Potter, known as "Fifi" to her close friends. Roadblocks had been placed by James Stillman's father, who thought his heir should have married into the Vanderbilt, Astor, or Whitney families. His daughters, Isabel and Elsie, had married Rockefellers, and he had visions of an equally prestigious marriage for his son.

Few were more aware than Stillman Sr. that the hierarchy

21

of American society was determined by wealth. Wealth meant power. This was true in towns or small cities where the mill owner, large merchant, banker, or ship owner was the leading citizen and his wife the leading lady. It was equally true in the big cities where wealth was the criterion of social position. And in New York the social pecking order was determined by *great* wealth.

But James Stillman, Jr., had an eye for beauty and refused to let his father select a wife for him on the basis of a bankbook. He had chosen Anne, whose family, though rich, was hardly in the Stillmans' monetary league. Over the angry objections of his father and the quiet protests of his mother, he married Anne.

The couple enjoyed an opulent lifestyle. Anne appreciated the finest in jewels, clothes, and homes, and her sense of style made her the envy of her contemporaries. She was the Jacqueline Kennedy Onassis of her day, and maintained her glamor, sparkle, and figure even after the birth of four children.

However, for seventeen years the elder Stillman never truly accepted Anne, and his death on March 15, 1918 was hardly the saddest day of her life.

Even without the blessings of the elder Stillman, James' and Anne's social life had been more or less normal. But among the rich in the early 1900s, "normal" was an umbrella word that covered a lot of territory.

High society condoned almost everything except public scandal or divorce. The rule was "Keep it quiet and you can do almost anything." At weekend parties in many city mansions and country estates the butler rang a bell at nine o'clock in the morning, and everyone went back to their own rooms. Do as you please was an accepted standard of conduct—the crime was not the conduct, but getting caught.

For society people in the early 1920s, divorce or public scandal was a fate worse than death, for in all but extremely rare instances it meant exclusion from the Social Register. That ended social life as effectively as the guillotine.

James A. Stillman, born in New York City on August 18, 1873, enjoyed all the advantages of being born with a golden spoon in his mouth. In his case it was encrusted with diamonds.

As a child James was easygoing and sociable, although he had a violent temper, which he was fortunately able to control. He maintained these traits throughout his early life and during four years at Harvard, where he was active in sports as the star pitcher on the baseball team and a highly valued member of the crew.

His temper, usually under control except under extreme provocation, resulted in a legend at Harvard. Upon returning from a practice drill on the Charles River, one of the members of the crew, John Anderson, made and repeated derogatory remarks about "Jim crapping up the rhythm of the crew." Angered at the second repetition of the remark, Stillman, possessed of enormous strength, lifted Anderson above his head and heaved him about five feet into the river. The story grew like a fishing tale, and within two weeks the halls of Harvard had Stillman throwing his crew mate halfway across the Charles River with one hand.

Upon graduation from Harvard in 1896, Stillman entered the employ of the National City Bank as a clerk. The formula for Stillman's promotion at the bank was simple—have a father who is president and the bank's largest stockholder. Superiors wisely saw the wisdom of recognizing qualities and overlooking deficiencies.

To no one's surprise Stillman rose in rapid steps to become executive manager of the bank, proving once again—if proof is needed—that the quickest road to the top is the proper choice of a father.

Stillman, now a Rockefeller in-law by virtue of the marriages of two sisters to Rockefellers, became president of the prestigious National City Bank in 1918 upon the death of his father. He was the most powerful banker in the country, except for J. Pierpont Morgan.

On July 9, 1920, he startled New York society, and the financial world, by starting an action for divorce just as his wife was about to leave for Paris on the White Star liner *Olympic*.

Stillman's sensational allegations and his wife's counter-charges titillated high society and the public, which made a Roman holiday of the washing of dirty linen by society leaders. There was plenty of linen, including the allegations that Stillman had affairs with ten different women, which was quite a tribute (or, in the opinion of some, not much of a tribute) to his virility. It would seem that he found plenty of time for activities other than banking.

Stillman spelled out the accusations of his wife's straying from the path of virtue. To the horror of the board of directors of the bank, he alleged that on May 1, 1917, Anne Stillman had had intercourse with an Indian guide, Fred Beauvais, an employee of the Stillman lodge at Three Rivers, Quebec. ("An Indian!" exclaimed the fast-dwindling ranks of the couple's friends.)

Stillman further alleged that this affair continued at various times and places in Canada, and even spilled over to Stillman's hallowed house in Pocantico Hills, the barony of the Rockefellers. These little excursions, said Stillman, resulted in the birth of a child, Guy, on November 22, 1918, and the father was, according to Stillman, Fred Beauvais.

Anne Stillman denied the charge—"A pack of lies!"—and requested the court to award her temporary alimony pending the outcome of the trial. In view of Stillman's financial ability the Court very generously awarded Anne seventy-five hundred dollars a month to soothe her injured feelings until a final determination of the case was made.

This might not be considered extraordinarily high by today's standards, but it was the largest award of temporary alimony made until that time. It was the equivalent of thirty thousand dollars a month in 1975.

Stillman countered his wife's application for alimony by attempting to introduce a letter Anne had written to him confessing her relations with the guide. But Justice Morschauser, who had been designated to hear the case, refused to consider it on the ground that communications between husband and wife are marital confidences and inadmissible.

The decision of the court was understandably very convenient for a temporarily elated Mrs. Stillman. However, two years later, on November 8, 1923, in an appeal to the Appellate Division to set aside the decision in the divorce action won by Anne, Stillman annexed the alleged confession letter, and it became public. The significant sentence everyone immediately noted was ". . . I was too proud to break, but I broke just the same in the arms of my Indian. . . ."

It was a rambling letter, but its tenor was very clear.

The commencement of divorce proceedings put Anne Stillman in a greatly depressed mood. Now that everything was in the open, whether the accusations were true or false meant little, for they were public, and that meant scandal. Headaches began to plague her. She had recurrent dreams of walking across Niagra Falls on a tightrope while people, who resembled her friends, threw rocks at her.

It was becoming more than she could bear, and she confided to a maid, "Life isn't really worthwhile." Alarmed, the maid telephoned Mrs. Katherine Mackay, a close friend of Anne's and a leading socialite. (Mackay's daughter Ellen married Irving Berlin and was thereafter ostracized by society, although Mrs. Mackay continued to be acknowledged as one of its leaders.)

Mrs. Mackay immediately came to see Anne, and it turned out to be an important visit. "Fifi, the world hasn't come to an end," she told her. "Stop pitying yourself and *fight*. Get busy or they'll push you over the dam."

Apparently Anne needed someone like Katherine Mackay to jolt her out of her depression and into action. She urged Anne to retain Stanchfield and Levy, one of the best-known law firms in the country. Anne protested, "I've already retained Cadwalader, Wickersham and Taft." This firm, too, was one of the top in the nation.

Mrs. Mackay's solution was the height of simplicity— retain them both. She knew the legal ropes. Having been through a divorce recently, she knew that James Stillman, and not Anne, would have to pay the lawyers. So why not get the best and the most?

From the time she employed Stanchfield and Levy as her counsel, Mrs. Stillman's defense speeded up. A corps of investigators went to work to get evidence against Mr. Stillman, to be used in the "affirmative defense" her lawyers decided to plead. This meant that instead of Anne's being merely a defendant, she would also make affirmative charges of infidelity against him. Instead of being just a punching bag, she was going to hit back. Under New York law at that time, if she could prove adultery on James Stillman's part, it would preclude his getting a divorce, even if he could prove misconduct on her part.

Affidavits were obtained making allegations of adultery against Stillman with Mrs. Florence Leeds, a former Ziegfeld Follies chorus girl. Anne then amended her answer to accuse her husband of infidelity and named him as the father of Jay Ward Leeds, the child of Florence Leeds.

The investigators were busy and efficient, for by May 8, 1921, they had come up with nine more women described as singers, dancers, and chorus girls who were said to have been intimately involved in what was apparently *La Dolce Vita* of "sedate" James Stillman. According to one of Anne's attorneys a supplemental answer would be made, and he promised, "It will be lurid enough to make all preceding papers in the case look pale by comparison."

The case was now heating up. The sensational allegations and the unusual evidence were front-page news throughout the country. They competed for headlines with Warren G. Harding, the newly elected President of the United States, who was soon to take his place in history in the Teapot Dome oil scandal.

Using the Stillman case as a subject, ministers thundered from their pulpits about morality and the wages of sin. Comedians in vaudeville seized upon it gleefully, saying that at seven thousand five hundred dollars a month the wages of sin were pretty good! The great wealth and social position of the Stillmans, and their relationship with the Rockefellers, the wealthiest family in the nation, made it a field day for humor, public and private. However, the involved parties weren't laughing.

The lawyers for both sides appeared before Justice Morschauser of the Supreme Court in Westchester County and requested that a referee be appointed to hear evidence. The court appointed Daniel J. Gleason, former surrogate of Dutchess County. Unbelievably, it would be June 2, 1925, almost five years after the action was commenced, before the case was finally decided by the Court of Appeals. They were five hectic years, filled with charges, countercharges, and allegations of adultery, bribery, forgery, and subornation of perjury.

Not long after the case became public in 1921, James Stillman became the first casualty of the legal war and resigned as president of the National City Bank. The question asked was rhetorical—"Was he pushed or did he fall?" It didn't much matter—the fact was, he was out. However, with a fortune estimated at fifty million dollars, he was hardly worried about paying the monthly bills.

The charges against Mrs. Stillman opened with a bang. French-Canadian witnesses were brought in to testify to various times and places of Anne's alleged indiscretions with Beauvais. They testified, eagerly and with a sense of importance, that they had listened at keyholes and used ladders to look in at windows. In one instance a ladder had fallen, causing noise and confusion, with window peepers running in all directions, but no one in the house had come out to see what had happened. In another, they went looking in the wrong window, and again the ladder fell. It had overtones of a Keystone Comedy, and all that was lacking was Mack Sennett.

Mrs. Stillman informed her attorneys that the keyhole and ladder testimony of the French-Canadian witnesses was manufactured. "Bought-and-paid-for testimony," was how she phrased it.

While this testimony was making headlines, Anne's friends were leaking news to the press about Mr. Stillman's affair with Florence Leeds. To add to the circus atmosphere, rumors began to circulate about the close friendship of Anne, age forty-one, and Harold Fowler McCormick, age twenty, who was usually called Fowler by his friends.

Fowler, a close friend of Anne's son Bud, was a student at Princeton, a grandson of John D. Rockefeller, and a first cousin of Nelson and David Rockefeller. On his paternal side, Fowler was the grandson of Cyrus McCormick, the inventor of the reaper, which had revolutionized wheat farming. He was heir to the International Harvester fortune, and the McCormick family was considered one of the three wealthiest in the nation.

Both Fowler and Anne denied any romance. However, six months before the divorce proceedings began, Anne had advised Stillman that she was in love with a young man well known in society and that she wished to get a divorce in France and marry him. Anne later changed her mind about a divorce. Then Stillman decided to get a divorce, naming as correspondent, not the young socialite, but the Indian guide Fred Beauvais.

The romance between a forty-one-year-old pillar of society and a twenty-year-old Rockefeller grandson startled a public that was growing accustomed to the bizarre in the Roaring Twenties era of the Great Gatsby. The addition of Beauvais and a blond, blue-eyed baby who was supposedly half-Indian made it all somewhat hard to swallow.

John D. Rockefeller, then eighty-three years old, was a moralist of the first magnitude, and the scandal involving his grandson angered and upset him. His anger was heightened when it was brought to his attention that the romance was being tossed around in public places. Will Rogers, the great American humorist, whom Rockefeller greatly admired, was poking fun at Fowler in his nightly act at the Ziegfeld Follies. Twirling his rope and talking in his inimitable drawl, Rogers would say, "Well, I understand that Anne Stillman says that her friendship with Fowler is platonic. I can't see why people won't accept that as the truth. It's platonic, all right. It's play for him and tonic for her!"

John D. Rockefeller's morality was not a sham. He neither drank, smoked, nor philandered. This man, who by ruthless and illegal methods wrecked business competitors, driving some to suicide and many to ruin, and engaged in the wholesale corruption of public officials, was the epitome of rectitude in matters relating to his family.

His personal morality apparently had its beginnings in the fact that his father, William Rockefeller, known as Big Bill, was a charlatan of the first order. He called himself Doctor William Rockefeller, Cancer Specialist, although he had never seen the inside of a medical school. He peddled bottles of colored water as medicine for all ailments at county fairs, and as a cancer cure to credulous farmers.

Big Bill had signs posted at village hotels, HERE FOR ONE DAY ONLY. ALL CASES OF CANCER CURED, UNLESS TOO FAR GONE, and offered treatments at two dollars. Showing acute Rockefeller wisdom, he stayed in one place for only one day—long enough to collect the sucker money but not long enough to be found when the yokels realized they had been taken.

Making enough from his cancer excursions to buy a house in Richford, New York, Rockefeller stayed home from his fleecing operations long enough to get himself into trouble with his neighbors and was accused of stealing horses.

In 1849 Big Bill got into big trouble with his housemaid, Ann Vanderbeak. He left the county one step ahead of the sheriff after Ann went to the district attorney with the story of Big Bill's forceful and unwelcome adventures in her attic bedroom, filing criminal charges.

His father's escapade with the housemaid apparently had a profound effect on John D. Rockefeller, for in his personal life, as related to sexual morality, there was never the slightest deviation from a straight line. He demanded the same of his children and grandchildren. In this way he somehow hoped to expiate the sins of his father.

But his sense of morality seemed to be badly warped when it came to business, for no one was more ruthless, and in dealings with public officials no one was more corrupt. This paragon of personal virtue saw nothing wrong with bribery to further his business interests. He saw nothing wrong in having legislators surreptitiously on the Standard Oil payroll. Others received bribes in the form of "loans," and a congressman, Joseph Sibley, served as the Standard Oil briber in both houses of Congress.

Sibley would write to the company at 26 Broadway, in New York City, "A Senator came to me today to make a loan. I told him I did not have it but would try to get it for him in a day or two. . . . Do you want to make the investment?"

"Loans" seemed to be a safe method of bribery, and senators and representatives received them in sums up to twenty-five thousand dollars. This was a tremendous amount at the time; the most highly skilled mechanic then earned two dollars per day, and schoolteachers received five dollars a week.

Throughout his life Rockefeller used bribery and corruption. His conscience never bothered him. But neither did he ever change his standard of personal virtue, and Fowler's fall from grace was a great shock.

Apparently Anne's law firms were finding it a little awkward with the elder Rockefeller now involved, for by a peculiar coincidence Stanchfield and Levy, and Cadwalader, Wickersham and Taft both withdrew from the case without a public explanation. Such action by two firms at one time was highly unusual. It was conjectured that influential clients, representing the most powerful financial and business interests in the country, forced the withdrawal of both in the hope of getting the case settled and off the front pages, since it was tarnishing the image not only of the Rockefellers, but of others who had great wealth and social position.

This put Anne in a difficult position. None of the prestigious New York law firms would now handle the case, and she was forced to retain counsel from outside the city. Again Katherine Mackay came to the rescue. She strongly recommended retaining John F. Brennan, an oustanding lawyer of Westchester County.

It was a happy choice, as he proved to be energetic, highly competent, and a master at the art of cross-examination.

At the hearings Stillman's sister, Mrs. Isabel Rockefeller, wife of Percy Rockefeller, took the stand for her brother. In a voice blurred by tears she cried throughout her testimony. What she was crying about, no one really understood.

"James Stillman could not be the father of Guy," she sobbed. "He was living, separated from Anne, at the home of my ill father during the possible months of conception of the child." In answer to a question by Stillman's attorney she said, still in tears, "I have seen him there daily."

A lengthy cross-examination brought out the weakness of her contention. Perhaps Mrs. Rockefeller saw Stillman every day, but she did not necessarily know where he went every night. Living at the home of his father at 9 East 72nd Street hardly prevented him from visiting Anne, whose home was not far away.

While Mrs. Rockefeller was testifying, and all during the cross-examination, Anne, with a pink bandanna around her bobbed hair, sat at the counsel table busily knitting. This seemed to disconcert Mrs. Rockefeller, and possibly that was its purpose. When asked what she was knitting, Anne smiled, smoothed an imaginary wrinkle in her skirt, and said, "It isn't what you think."

The Stillman testimony thus far was not going too badly against Anne. Although it hardly portrayed her as Rebecca of

Sunnybrook Farm, nothing really conclusive had been shown that could not be explained or denied. And then a bomb burst, with a doctor's testimony, which seemed to all but wreck her hopes.

Doctor Hugh Russell, an osteopath from Buffalo, New York, was a long-time family friend and doctor to the Stillmans. He was tense as he commenced his testimony, and his nervous smile flashed on and off, much like a neon light. He testified that while seeing him for treatment in April 1918, six months before Guy's birth, Anne had told him, "James Stillman is not the father of this child. Fred Beauvais is the father." A collective gasp ran through the spectators.

The doctor's testimony was of double importance—it had bearing on the divorce action and on the legitimacy of Guy for purposes of inheritance under a seven million dollar trust set up by Stillman's father for the benefit of the children of Stillman and Anne.

The testimony was admitted after a bitter legal battle between counsel that lasted for three hours. Anne's attorney used every effort to get Referee Gleason to exclude it on the ground that a conversation between a doctor and a patient was privileged.

However, Stillman's attorneys contended that although the law regards conversations with a priest or lawyer as privileged, it accords some leeway to a physician by prescribing that only that part of a conversation between a patient and a physician is privileged which is necessary for treatment of the case. The phraseology of the statute, it was asserted, practically permits the physician to be the judge of what he considers privileged. Stillman's attorney argued that Dr. Russell had opened the door for his testimony when he declared that what Anne had told him was not necessary for her treatment.

Doctor Russell was finally permitted to testify concerning

his conversation with Mrs. Stillman after he stated for the record that the information she had given him had not been necessary for the treatment of her case.

John E. Mack, the special guardian for Guy, then obtained a ruling from the referee that the testimony was not competent insofar as the issue of Guy's paternity was concerned.

Mr. Mack raised the point that under the terms of the statute neither parent was competent to testify in an illegitimacy proceeding. For that reason, Mack contended, Anne's alleged confession to Doctor Russell should be incompetent in the paternity issue, even if established, although it might be considered in the divorce action.

The admission of the doctor's testimony was devastating to Anne. Here was a supposedly friendly, unbiased doctor, with no apparent motive to testify falsely, giving testimony that was a hammer blow to her case.

The court permitted Dr. Russell to continue his testimony the next day, and a cross-examination that lasted two hours did not shake him in the least. As a matter of form, after Russell stepped down from the witness stand, Anne's attorney made a motion to strike out all of his testimony, with no expectation, in view of the referee's previous ruling, that it would be granted. At this point a recess was called.

Anne was standing in the hall outside the courtroom, talking with counsel and friends. A spectator remarked to a friend, "Confession may be good for the soul, but it certainly is bad for her case." That seemed to sum it up.

Anne's world appeared to be crumbling, and she didn't believe the words used to try to cheer her up, possibly because the people saying them did not believe them. Life now seemed to be an endless climb on a steep, slippery slope. It was a glum and disheartened group of counsel and friends that walked into the courtroom after the recess.

The referee returned to the bench, and then came the stunning announcement. Without giving a reason for his ruling, he granted the motion to strike out completely the testimony of Dr. Russell.

In disbelief Anne looked at her attorneys, who looked as unbelieving as she did. The agony she had undergone at the testimony turned into ecstasy at the decision. In sheer jubilation she could hardly restrain herself from embracing her lawyers. But they were too dignified for that, and even in her bewildered state she realized that it would embarrass them. As she said later, "I didn't know whether I was going to faint, laugh, cry, dance, or sing."

But she had to do something. She was bursting. So she walked, then ran, to a friend wearing a bright red polka-dotted dress, sitting in the front row of spectators, embraced her, and held on tightly. Anne would have sworn that when she was talking to her in the hall, a few minutes before, the dress had been dark. Now, she realized, it was bright red. But the whole world had changed in the last few minutes. Everything was now bathed in bright colors, and life seemed very much worth living.

The referee could almost feel the vibrations from the participants and spectators, and he wisely decided not to call another witness. Since it was then three o'clock he adjourned the case until the following day.

As an aftermath of Dr. Russell's testimony, a movement was started in the Osteopathic Society to oust him for unethical conduct. He was criticized for an apparent breach of professional ethics in a statement issued by a majority of the directors of the New York State Osteopathic Society.

An announcement was made that charges had been filed against him and that he probably would be expelled from the Society. The case against him started with a roar and ended in a whisper. Nothing happened.

The divorce proceedings brought a division of loyalty among the Stillman children. There was animosity and hostility between the two eldest. Bud, the seventeen-year-old son, sided with the mother, and Anne, the nineteen-year-old daughter, gave her allegiance to Stillman. "Anne is out for herself," said Bud. "She was influenced by the Rockefellers. I tried to talk to her, but a girl of nineteen does not like to take advice from her younger brother."

Alexander, the third child, although only ten and supposedly too young to comprehend the proceedings, aggressively sided with the mother. He appeared at the trial, and at a well-planned dramatic moment he lifted three-year-old Guy into the witness chair to be looked at and spoken to by the referee.

On May 9, 1921, the tall, broad-shouldered Bud met the elder Stillman by chance in the lobby of the Plaza Hotel in Manhattan. An angry confrontation took place. Bud asked his father to drop the suit, and Stillman quickly replied, "No, I am going through with it. I started it, and I intend to finish it. What's done is done and can't be undone." Bud said to his shocked parent, "Why? For years you've been living with other women. Everyone seems to know it. You didn't even try to hide it."

Trying to control himself, Stillman said, "That's not true. I have never in my life lived with any woman but your mother."

Bud said heatedly, "That's a lie, and you know it. And I

don't give a damn what you think about Guy. He's my brother, and nothing you say is going to change that."

Stillman, visibly shaken at the venomous feeling obvious in the voice and manner of his son, walked away, giving a baleful look to a gathering group of curious onlookers.

"It never came to blows," Bud said later. "I'd like to have, all right, but I'm glad it didn't. I guess it wouldn't have been the right thing to do."

As the case progressed, however, there seemed to be a change of heart on the part of the daughter. Time apparently had a healing effect in the rupture between the mother and her eldest child. When this took place or why, no one but Anne seemed to know, and she wasn't talking about it. But when it happened Anne rented a sixteen-room apartment for herself and a fourteen-room apartment for her daughter, both at 910 Fifth Avenue. The rental for both apartments was thirty-seven thousand dollars annually, in 1921 dollars. Anne really knew how to live. It's not difficult, when some one else is paying for it.

Stillman was the final witness in the plaintiff's case, but he far from covered himself with glory. He gave all the testimony necessary to fill out his case against Anne. But on cross-examination about his relationship with Florence Leeds and other women, he faltered. He refused to answer the astounding total of 423 questions, on the ground that "to do so would tend to incriminate me," being careful to avoid using the word "degrade," which is usually coupled with "incriminate" in the legal phrase.

Stillman owned the yacht *Modesty*, and Anne's attorney asked him, "Who christened the yacht?"

"I refuse to answer."

"On what ground?"

"It might tend to incriminate me."

"Was the yacht *Modesty* christened by Florence Leeds?"

"I refuse to answer on the ground it might tend to incriminate me."

"Did you purchase an apartment on Park Avenue for Mrs. Leeds?"

"I refuse to answer on the same grounds as before."

"Did you own a home in Miami, Florida, occupied by Mrs. Leeds?"

"I refuse to answer on the same grounds as before."

"Did you visit her there?"

"I refuse to answer on the same grounds as before."

"Was it called the Love Nest?"

"I refuse to answer on the same grounds as before."

"Did you live with Florence Leeds as your wife?"

"I refuse to answer on the same grounds."

"Did you create a trust fund in the amount of one million dollars for Jay Leeds?"

"I refuse to answer on the same grounds."

"While you were in Atlantic City with your family in 1918 did you maintain an apartment with a woman other than Florence Leeds in another hotel?"

"I refuse to answer on the same grounds."

The cross-examination continued on Stillman's relations with Florence Leeds and nine other women. He refused to answer hundreds of questions, always on the ground that "to do so would tend to incriminate me." But even with his refusal to answer the story was coming out, and the effect of his refusal to answer was devastating.

On Stillman's rebuttal after cross-examination the attorney rested his case.

Stillman's exit from the courthouse led to a lighter moment. Wishing to avoid photographers, reporters, and motion-picture cameras assembled in front of the courthouse steps, he was guided by a building attendant to an exit in the cellar that led to the rear of the building.

Climbing over pipes, boxes, and lumber strewn about in the cellar, he tripped and fell into a coal pile. Rising, he again fell over loose coal, and the fall caused more coal to cascade down from the pile. Thoroughly dirty, grimy, and disheveled, the usually immaculate banker emerged through the cellar door to be met by, "Hello, Mr. Stillman," and a cheery group of newsreel cameramen and reporters.

Apparently a ten dollar payment to the right person had saved the press a lot of wondering about where Mr. Stillman would emerge.

Now Anne's defense was to have its day in court. The strategy was simple. She would explain what could be explained and deny what could not. The major theme was to admit nothing, and her whole case was to be orchestrated as a variation on this theme.

Anne called a total of thirty-two persons to refute the testimony of Stillman's witnesses and place her alleged actions in an innocent context. Under cross-examination they stood up very well.

Anne's lawyers had made every possible objection to exclude damaging written evidence and had succeeded with the most important item, the "confession" letter, which had not been permitted into evidence. However, there were four affectionately worded letters, allegedly written by Anne to Fred Beauvais, for which a private detective, Edmund Leight, testified he had paid fifteen thousand dollars to the Indian guide. Although Beauvais denied he had sold them, James Sheehan, a reporter for the *New York Daily News*, testified that he had been present at the sale.

As part of the plaintiff's case, these letters had been accepted by the Court and marked as Exhibits 80, 81, 82, and 83. They were part of the record. Anne cut that Gordian knot by calmly proclaiming them forgeries. She said that if Stillman had indeed bought them he had purchased worthless pieces of paper. Anne was a superb witness. Later, Mr. Stillman's attorney grudgingly conceded that she had been "excellent."

Having conducted herself brilliantly as a witness, Anne now proceeded on her "affirmative defense," to counterattack with proof of Stillman's misconduct, with a "look who was talking" approach. If she could prove misconduct on Stillman's part, regardless of her own conduct, Stillman could not obtain a divorce.

Florence Leeds first meet Stillman in October 1917. A member of the Ziegfeld Follies chorus, she was outstanding even in that group of elite beauties. When she first met Stillman she believed him to be a bachelor, but when she later learned that he was married her feelings for him were not changed by that slight technicality. The fact that he was a leading banker who showered her with jewels and money did not seem to lessen her affections. As she later confided to a friend, "It is just as easy to fall in love with a rich man as a poor one."

Very shortly after the relationship began, Flo was installed in an apartment at 64 East 86th Street, and later in a luxuriously furnished twelve-room cooperative duplex at 969 Park Avenue. Mrs. Leeds said she purchased the duplex with money she saved from her Stillman allowance. However, although Stillman was far from miserly with her, it was quite a feat of financial wizardry to save enough to purchase a Park Avenue plush duplex worth $160,000 on a $1,500 monthly allowance.

The relationship was not flamboyant. In an interview Mrs. Leeds said, "My life with Mr. Stillman was very quiet. It was no wild romance, and I was not a bedtime toy. We were very congenial, and Mr. Stillman kept me secluded, as if I were a wife. I did not care, because I honestly and truly loved him, and I thought he loved me."

The contrast between this self-portrait and the picture painted by Anne's investigators and attorneys would have made it very confusing for the public to judge whether Flo was a sinner or a saint, if her self-evaluation had received wide publicity. But it never did, and the beating drums of the press carried the message that Florence was Jezebel! Jezebel! Jezebel!

Anne tried in every way to subpoena Florence as a witness, but Florence was most elusive. Later, Mrs. Leeds said that Stillman had sent her to places all over the country, and out of the country, to avoid service. Many times she had eluded process servers by minutes, and in one instance she had left in a car less than thirty seconds before they entered the lobby of her building.

In a way Anne was not unhappy that Mrs. Leeds, a stunningly beautiful woman, did not appear. The last thing at this point Anne wanted was to have the depressing feeling of "Well, you can't blame him for wanting something like that!"

Having failed to produce Mrs. Leeds, Anne's attorney proceeded with proof of Flo's relationship with Stillman. Martha Hays, a beautician, testified that Mrs. Leeds had been coming to her place of business since the latter part of 1919. She was impressed with the amount and quality of the jewels Florence wore and her general aura of "style and class." Martha stated that she became aware after a few months that Mrs. Leeds was pregnant and that she had gone to the Sloane Maternity Hospital to give her beauty treatments after the birth of her child.

Miss Hays further testified that two weeks after Mrs. Leeds left the hospital, she was called to her home at 64 East 86th Street, and after administering a beauty treatment, she had been introduced by Mrs. Leeds to a Mr. Leeds. Thereafter she had seen him at the house a few times.

A few weeks later she had visited Mrs. Leeds at the Plaza Hotel to give beauty treatments and there met Mr. Leeds again. Asked if she recognized Mr. Leeds in the courtroom, she rose, looked slowly around the room, pointed at James Stillman, and said, "That is Mr. Leeds!"

Anne's attorneys then proceeded to tighten the noose. They submitted evidence to prove that James A. Stillman and "Franklin Harold Leeds" were the same person. They called to the witness stand a subpoenaed clerk of the Motor Vehicle Bureau.

In an application for an automobile license made by James A. Stillman the following description of the applicant appeared:

> Age 45 years, white, male, 170 pounds, 5 feet 11 inches, brown hair, blue eyes, astigmatic, operated a car 10 years, driven 50,000 miles.

In an application for an automobile license made by Franklin Harold Leeds there was the following:

> Age 45 years, white, male, 170 pounds, 5 feet 11 inches, brown hair, blue eyes, astigmatic, operated a car 10 years, driven 50,000 miles.

As the clerk intoned the identical descriptions some of the

spectators could not contain their laughter. This was quickly stopped by the referee.

Stillman was obviously upset, and with a glare he rudely pushed back a note his attorney had handed him.

The hearings were over. The case to date had cost Stillman $729,000 in legal fees and payments to Anne. The hearings had been long and bitter, and there were almost seven thou sand pages of testimony for the Referee to consider. The ordeal of waiting for a decision was about to begin, and it would be more than four months before the decision was handed down.

The tension of daily attendance at the proceedings, and preparation on those days when there were no hearings, had kept Anne in a constant state of tension. Now that it was over, there was a tremendous letdown, and it left her limp.

She now had time to think of the past and the future. She knew that her life could never be the same. The hypocrisy of society, which condemned those publicly accused of infidelity but condoned adultery as a way of life in private, made her bitter. She realized only too well that she had previously accepted this double standard, and had never given more than a passing thought to those caught in the web of deceit. But in doing so she had merely conformed to the mores of her peers.

The winds of social acceptance of infidelity had not blown over the United States in the 1920s. While Continental Europe accepted indiscretion with almost a shrug, and mistresses and lovers as a fact of life, American morality in the public conduct of most married persons was on a plane that would have met the approval of that paragon of morality, Queen Victoria.

With a smile Anne recalled to her friend Constance Ewing

a tea at which the question of infidelity had been raised, and the hilarity with which the guests had received comments on the subject by Mrs. Vanderbilt, the hostess.

Mrs. Vanderbilt said she had heard that the stone lions, sedately squatting on their haunches in front of the Astor Library on Fifth Avenue and 42nd Street, stood up and roared whenever a member of either sex of the Four Hundred passed who was faithful to their marriage vows. When she observed dryly, "The lions haven't roared yet!" the laughter was uncontrollable. Then, remembered Anne, "one of the guests, with a straight face, said that quite a number of her friends had heard the story and avoided passing the Astor Library."

In discussions with her friends, Anne almost compulsively dwelt on the subject of false pretension. The basis of the hypocrisy, she said, was the image high society had to maintain. She reflected that the self-annointed upper crust could not admit to any of the defects and blemishes of lesser mortals. The inside of the cup might be tarnished, but the outside that was viewed by the world had to be polished and shining. It mattered little what the facts actually were, "it was what they seemed to be that mattered."

Anne knew those were the rules, and nothing she could do would change them. She realized that even if she was completely successful in her defense, exonerated of any wrongdoing by the Court, the damage had been done. Her life was as shattered as a broken vase. And like a vase, although it could be mended, it would never be the same. The stares, the pointed fingers, the thoughts and whispers of people were something no decision of any court could control.

But life had to go on. Anne had her family and a few close friends. She was not invited to any social functions, but that did not bother her because she would have rejected any invitations. The most insensitive person would have felt ill-at-ease in attending a function under these circumstances. A sensitive person would have found it almost impossible, and Anne was very sensitive. She would have felt that she was on exhibition.

Anne's troubles, however, were not without a lighter side and prospective monetary value. Two weeks after the hearings ended, Biograph Films offered her a hundred thousand dollars to appear in two pictures. They did not bother to ask whether she had ever acted or even could act. They assumed that if she could not act, whatever drama they put her in would become an unintentional comedy, as has happened many times when the public has viewed a picture and laughed in places the producer never intended and the actor never expected. They felt certain the public would flock, not to see the picture, but to view the well-publicized Anne U. Stillman. They never did find out whether Anne could act; she wisely turned down the offer.

On September 29, 1922, Referee Daniel J. Gleason handed down the long-awaited findings, and they were confirmed by Justice Morschauser on October 6. The decision read, ". . . The learned Referee in this case found, decided, and reported that the testimony did not justify a finding of adultery against the defendant, Anne U. Stillman, and also that the defense of plaintiff's adultery was established, and also that the infant defendant, Guy Stillman, was the legitimate child of the plaintiff and the defendant, Anne U. Stillman. . . ."

Anne received the news of her victory in Canada. She was on her yacht, hurrying down the St. Maurice River to obtain medical help for Guy, who was ill at the Stillman camp at Grand Anse.

A correspondent for the Canadian press boarded the yacht

from a tug and handed Anne a copy of the press release reporting the decision. After reading it she was deeply affected. "It is a victory of tears," she said. "So much pain for others. My father dead, my family hurt, and my children with a marked name. I cannot be gay. It is all too deep for joy."

Asked if a reconciliation might be possible, she replied, "There is a French word which will be my answer. *Jamais.*"

Anne then castigated Stillman. "A man who does not acknowledge his own child is an outcast. However, Mr. Stillman is not as bad as one would think. He has been ill-advised by bad friends. I entreated him to part company with that girl Florence Leeds. Here he was, the president of the biggest bank in America, led by that girl and badly neglecting his business."

Asked whether she would now divorce Stillman, she said, "Never! Mr. Stillman would then get married to Florence and legitimatize her children to the detriment of mine. And I will never go back to live with him. Never!"

However, Anne knew her war was far from over. She felt absolutely certain an appeal would be taken and it would be some time before a final determination would be made.

Upon returning to New York she conferred with her lawyers and decided to make an application to increase her temporary alimony from seventy-five hundred to ten thousand dollars a month so that she could await further developments in even greater comfort.

Justice Morschauser, however, had different thoughts on that subject. He felt that seventy-five hundred dollars a month was sufficient to keep Anne living in a style to which she was accustomed and which the wealth of her husband permitted. He denied the application for the increase.

To add to Stillman's troubles, Flo Leeds now threatened to sue him for support of the child she claimed he had fathered.

She said that Stillman was no longer sending her monthly checks and the infant might become a public charge.

Flo called a press conference and repeated the statement to fifteen reporters assembled in the plush surroundings of her duplex apartment on Park Avenue. That anyone in that apartment could become a public charge excited some of the reporters to polite laughter.

Mrs. Leeds told the newsmen that Mrs. Stillman had offered to take her son into her home and bring him up. Although she appreciated the offer, Flo said, "My son is *my* son, and I propose to raise him. I would like to thank Mrs. Stillman from the bottom of my heart, but I believe Mr. Stillman will do the right thing and provide for my boy's support. If he does not we still have courts in this land."

A reporter questioned Mrs. Stillman about her offer to bring up Flo's son. "I really did not make a direct offer to Mrs. Leeds to adopt Jay," said Anne, "but I would be glad to make such an offer. He is my son's half-brother, and if Mr. Stillman does not accept any responsibility for him, we do. I would bring the boy up as one of us. Of course, I know a child is always best off with his mother. Nothing, no matter how much you try, can supplant mother love, but I am certain that he hasn't a chance in the world to turn out well where he is."

Anne paused and thought for a moment, then continued, "She says she will not accept. I am sorry, for I really believe there isn't anyone in the world—his mother, Mr. Stillman, and his sisters included—who has more to offer the boy than I have. I would like to adopt Jay. Win or not win, licked or not licked, I am for Jay. He may not have his father behind him, but he has his three half-brothers and myself behind him. Slang sometimes hits the nail on the head better than anything else—I'll just say, 'Go to it, Flo Leeds. Do it!' "

In the glow of victory Anne had changed her mind and

lost her detestation of Flo. In fact, she had a feeling of great sympathy for her, and both were now united in a common bond of animosity toward Stillman. They saw each other quite frequently, and since neither now considered the other a rival for Stillman's affections, wife and mistress each used the other as a sounding board in venting her anger at an absent husband and lover. As a victorious veteran of legal battles, Anne advised Flo to go after Stillman for the support of the son fathered by him, and to "fight him like a tiger." She was obviously giving her former rival a page out of her own book.

On March 15, 1924, the Appellate Division in a unanimous decision affirmed Justice Morschauser's confirmation of the findings.

However, they directed that the finding of the Referee absolving Mrs. Stillman of wrongdoing be stricken from the report. The decision pointed out that this was immaterial, inasmuch as the finding that Stillman was guilty of adultery, and therefore not entitled to a judgment of divorce, was not dependent on a finding that Anne was innocent of wrongdoing.

This, lawyers pointed out, thrust back on Anne the burden of defending herself, if in later filing a divorce action against Stillman she was met by a countercharge.

Anne was in high spirits at the decision, even with the deletion. When reporters went to her home at Fifth Avenue and 72nd Street to get her reaction to the victory, she said she "felt as if I had been through a football game." A reporter for the New York *Daily News* asked, "Do you mean after scoring the winning touchdown?" She laughed and said, "The game isn't over yet. He still has the Court of Appeals."

It was pointed out to Anne that it was extremely rare for

a defeated litigant to be granted permission to carry an appeal from a unanimous decision of the Appellate Division. She replied, smiling, "I see you don't know my husband very well. He'll get permission and appeal."

She was right. Permission was granted, and Stillman took the case to the Court of Appeals.

From the time of the confirmation in Anne's favor by Justice Morschauser in October 1922, Fowler McCormick, "the best pal of my son Bud," had been a frequent guest at Anne's home in the Canadian woods. The visits were discreet and not publicized, and very few persons outside Anne's household knew of them.

However, in March 1925, while the case was before the Court of Appeals, Anne visited Fowler in Milwaukee and made no attempt to hide it. Tongues began to wag. Was the romance on again? Was she going to marry him? Was he going to marry her?

Fowler was working as a laborer in the International Harvester Plant, where he was learning the business from the ground up. "Of course, I found the work hard at first but I'm getting used to it now, and I like it," said Fowler, displaying well-callused hands. "They show I've been busy working, really working."

"Last night Fowler and I had dinner together," Anne told friends. "But the poor boy was so tired that even his eyes drooped with fatigue. And his hands—imagine, hands that never did harder work than grasp a steering wheel before— were totally callused."

Anne now became a little apprehensive. With the decision soon to be handed down by the state's highest court, she was afraid that any undue publicity might hurt her case, and she abruptly left Milwaukee.

A friend of Anne's, a lawyer, told her that her fears of the Court of Appeals were groundless, since that Court would determine the appeal solely on the basis of the written record and would not consider anything not in that record. Nevertheless, said Anne, "I'm not taking any chances."

On June 2, 1925, the Court of Appeals, in a unanimous decision held that Stillman had lost his right to a divorce by his own misconduct. They also held the accusations against Mrs. Stillman were ruled out as immaterial to the appeal, and that this decision did not pass on the guilt or innocence of Anne in the charges made by her husband.

Anne was elated at the final determination of the case but somewhat depressed that the Court had not ruled on her innocence. But she did feel a lot better when Katherine Mackay said, "Fifi, be thankful. Imagine how James must feel." She could just imagine!

On October 20, 1925, Anne started an action for divorce, utilizing the testimony of the Stillman trial as the basis for the action. Referee Gleason's findings, confirmed by Justice Morschauser, had found Stillman guilty of adultery. Since this had been sustained by the Appellate Division and the Court of Appeals, it seemed that Anne had a powerful case. The only fly in the ointment was that she faced the same dilemma that had confronted Stillman. If he could prove misconduct on her part, no matter what she proved against him, Anne would not get a divorce. Stillman's insurmountable problem in his case was now her problem. And its dimensions were no less formidable.

Immediately after Anne started her divorce action Fred Beauvais decided the time was ripe to engage in a little legal battle of his own. He had made unsuccessful efforts to have

Anne compensate him seventy-five hundred dollars for time lost aiding her in fighting her case three years before. She had ignored his requests, he said, and he now had no alternative but to sue.

He started legal action in Canada, since she had a home there. Anne interposed a defense, contending that "Beauvais, far from helping in defendant's case against her husband, was disloyal toward defendant and did seriously damage defendant's interests by selling to agents of her husband for the sum of fifteen thousand dollars letters which he claimed were written and addressed to him by defendant and which were forgeries."

However, Anne's lawyers were fearful of apple carts being upset. There was no telling what might come out in anger in a courtroom, and they felt that discretion at this time was the better part of valor. Concerned about the Stillman case, they persuaded Anne to settle the Beauvais claim the day before the case came up for trial.

Beauvais, apparently now feeling that the law courts were a fertile field to be plowed, started an action against Stillman for five hundred thousand dollars for libel, slander, and defamation of character.

As one wit remarked, "Fred Beauvais apparently has become a 'Sioux,' spelled S-U-E, Indian."

James Stillman was in a somewhat similar situation with Flo Leeds as Anne had been with Beauvais. With a divorce trial coming up, one of the last things Stillman wanted was to have Flo appearing as a witness against him. He realized that that was a strong possibility in view of the way she felt about his ignoring their infant son.

It was no great surprise, therefore, when an announcement was made by William M. Sullivan, who acted as Stillman's personal attorney, that the child had been provided for. "I was appointed trustee and guardian for the boy, and I intend to see to it that he is afforded every advantage and opportunity a youngster should have."

Sullivan made known that Jay would receive $20,000 a year until his twenty-first birthday, at which time he would receive an additional lump sum of $150,000.

Immediately after this information was made public Flo Leeds announced that she was leaving for Paris to be married to "a businessman." This would take her out of the country at the time of any possible trial of Anne's divorce action. The legal maneuvering had begun, and Stillman was protecting his flanks.

When it was time to answer Anne's complaint, Stillman's attorneys secured an extension of thirty days. When they secured a second extension rumors began to fly around like swirling autumn leaves that a reconciliation was in the making. Anne's reply to her friends about the rumors was, "Too much has been said and done to make it possible. And I am not one of those who turns the other cheek."

However, when enterprising newsmen confirmed that Mr. Stillman had purchased at Cartier's a $750,000 diamond necklace, which was delivered to Anne and not returned, the rumors seemed to have a basis in fact.

For Stillman the rationale of a reconciliation was simple. Time had had a healing effect, and the anger and the emotional trauma of the last five years had softened. Anne was still a very attractive woman, and for social and business reasons marriage had a place in the Stillman scheme of things. He had always philandered, and he held the Continental view that a mistress or two were a way of life. He believed that variety was spice for a spouse and made for a happier marriage. (He would not agree, of course, that the reasoning held equally true for the wife.)

There was also the matter of practicality. To date fees and disbursement paid to his lawyers, to Anne's, and to the guardian appointed for Guy had amounted to the stupendous sum of $942,000. In addition, he was paying Anne $90,000 a year in temporary alimony. In the event of further litigation the legal fees might amount to an equivalent sum, and if Anne were successful it was not improbable that she would be awarded double her present alimony.

Stillman was also tired. The strain of continued litigation had taken a good deal out of him, and he did not relish the thought of five more years of trial and appeals. Anne had been held guiltless by a Referee in spite of evidence that seemed overwhelming, and there was no guarantee that another referee would look at the matter differently.

Anne, on the other hand, had her problems with a reconciliation. She had been splashed with dirty water, besmirched, defamed. Turning the other cheek was not her style. She had said, "I am not the type that can be hit over the head one minute and then give in when told, 'Come kiss me, honey.'"

But she had to be practical. There was no certainty that she would be successful in her suit. Proving Stillman an adulterer would not necessarily win her case this time as it had the last. She now had the burden of freeing herself of that taint. Another Referee *might* look differently at the evidence.

Anne also had something else to worry about. In an interview with John B. Kennedy, published in *Collier's* magazine on February 6, 1926, Justice Morschauser came out strongly against divorce. "Divorce must go," said the jurist. "We have to abolish divorce just as we legally abolished booze."

Would the judge's expressed personal feelings carry over into his rulings in the courtroom? Anne felt that his integrity was such that it would not. But could she take the chance?

If the findings went against her, she would be up the creek financially.

The only other possibility for a successful divorce—that Stillman would not contest the case and would make a money settlement—was out. Stillman was adamant on that score.

Practicality won. The maneuvering toward the reconciliation had taken on aspects of two world powers engaged in a peace conference to end an international war. Emissaries were shuttling back and forth between the Stillmans, smoothing over minor differences so that the principals could meet in a summit conference. Gifts from Stillman to Anne were almost daily, and the $750,000 gift showed that negotiations were approaching a climax.

Anne had been warned about seeing her husband personally. Her lawyers had advised her that there was danger of jeopardizing her rights if she took any action that might be interpreted as condoning Stillman's alleged offenses. Her return to her husband, even if a reconcilation should prove short-lived, would wipe out the past and make it impossible for her ever to prosecute the divorce proceedings.

Nathan Miller, former Govenor of New York and now Stillman's chief negotiator, came to Anne with the message that perhaps meant more than all the gifts. "You are the only woman in the world, and nothing can fill the gap caused by your loss."

It was a reconciliation of convenience. Each had their own reasons. But the war was over. Or was it?

On February 6, 1926, James and Anne Stillman were aboard the White Star liner *Olympic* on the way to France. Reconciled! A second honeymoon. Two lovebirds on the way to a French love nest.

(By a curious coincidence they sailed on the ship on which Anne had been served papers in the divorce suit started by Stillman almost six years before. She had been in her state-room on that day in July 1920 when a process server handed her the papers that started the legal proceedings.)

They spent three months in France. Anne later told Katherine Mackay, "I honestly made every effort to make it work. We were happy for a while, and James acted like a newlywed. We went to the best psychiatrists in the world, including Sigmund Freud, to try and undo the trauma of all that had gone on in the courts. I was willing to forgive, but it was almost impossible to forget."

The Stillmans returned to New York on May 6, 1926, again on the *Olympic*. They were met on the boat by eighteen reporters and photographers.

Asked by the newsmen if the reconciliation with his wife was complete and if the second honeymoon had been as happy as anticipated, Stillman replied, "It was inevitable fate that things should happen as they have—fate or what-ever you wish to call it—but it has turned out wonderfully and most beautifully."

Anne was then asked if she believed her husband's atten-tion to business had been the cause of their previously drifting apart. She replied, "That American businessmen should be so occupied with business matters is hard on their wives. They don't give them enough attention. They give them money. They give them trips abroad. They give them everything they want but themselves, and *that* is what every woman wants. The women are lonely."

"How did European husbands compare with Americans?" a reporter inquired.

Anne laughed and said, "American husbands are much

better, and American wives more fortunate in their domestic relations than European women."

She paused for a moment and then continued, "A good English wife is no more than a respectable housekeeper. She is little better than his favorite horse or dog. The American husband will at least let his wife take a trip and buy herself some clothes, but the English husband feels it is a big deal if he lets his wife go for a ride on the bus."

"What of French husbands?"

"Oh, they're a bunch of bandits."

Everyone laughed.

"Mrs. Stillman," said a reporter, "we understand that your husband is really charming when he's in the mood. But we also know he has quite a temper. What is he like when he has that temper?"

"Well," said Anne smiling, looking at Stillman, "try and imagine Genghis Khan with a toothache. That will give you an idea!"

Four months later Stillman bought the elegant twenty-eight-room John Sherman Hoyt home at Park Avenue and 79th Street, for $1,500,000. That made page 5 of the newspapers. Mr. and Mrs. Stillman, except for occasional mention in the society columns, were out of the press.

One June 6, 1931, headlines screamed ANNE STILLMAN MARRIES FOWLER MC CORMICK!

Anne had obtained the final decree in a divorce on the morning of June 4 and had married Fowler on the afternoon of the same day!

The divorce proceedings had been a well-kept secret. A friend of Anne's, Alice Horton, gave the details to newsmen.

Anne had begun her suit early in November 1930. The case came up before Justice Morschauser on January 30, 1931 but was adjourned to February 6. Then, at a Special Term of the court, convened at the very unusual hour of 3 P.M., the testimony of a single witness, James Earl, was taken. An interlocutory decree was issued by Justice Morschauser on February 21. This decree became final on June 4.

Neither the former banker nor Anne testified at the brief hearing. Although it was public, not a single spectator was present. For some reason, perhaps a monetary gift, the court attendants did not divulge the proceedings to the press.

Five years previously, before her reconcilation with her husband, Anne had vehemently denied rumors that she planned to marry Fowler. "Of course we're not going to be married. We have been too good friends for that. Wouldn't it be ridiculous for a woman of forty-five—I am not imperishable, you know—to be the wife of a young man of twenty-four? I am too old and he is too young."

Everyone had more or less assumed that the romance had gone with the wind. But apparently it had been in dormant bloom during the years.

The wedding had taken place at Pleasantville, New York. Anne's thoughts about the age difference had obviously changed. She was now fifty years old, and Fowler was twenty-nine. To a friend, who undiplomatically asked, "Fifi, aren't you too old for him?" she had answered, "Apparently he doesn't think so."

The Stillman war was finally ended.

Tommy Manville
and
His Eleven Wives

On a sweltering New York day in August 1911, two excited young people on their way to obtain a marriage license gaily clambered onto a clanging horse-drawn trolley car at Third Avenue and 24th Street.

There were no photographers pressing for pictures, no reporters requesting intimate details. Tommy Manville, seventeen, and Florence Huber, four years older, were total unknowns to the world at large. They boarded the trolley and began a thirty-five-minute journey that resulted in the initial pealing of those fabled wedding bells that Manville, over the next forty-nine years, was to hear so often.

Tommy married his eleventh wife on January 12, 1960. By the time of the eleventh wedding, great changes had taken place in the world. There were no more horse-drawn trolleys, and jet planes spanned the Atlantic in six hours. Remaining constant over the decades, however, were the specifications of Manville wives. They were always the three Bs: Blonde, Busty, and Beautiful.

The time span of a Manville marriage was always a guessing

game and a gamble. But one union almost defied all odds.
It lasted an entire eight hours! This marriage, number seven,
caused Al Jolson to remark, "Tommy, if all you want is a
bottle of milk, why do you have to buy the cow?"

Thomas Franklin Manville, Jr., began life on August 14,
1894, the son of the founder and chairman of the Johns-
Manville Corporation. His parents were divorced in 1909.
The Court awarded custody of Tommy's sister, Lorraine, to
the mother, and Tommy was to be in custody of his father
until he reached twenty-one.

As a child he was stubborn, with strong likes and dislikes,
and once he had made up his mind, right or wrong, nothing
could change it. He detested school from the first day, and
after that his love of learning went downhill. Tommy and
formal education parted company when he ran away from
boarding school in 1910. His father located him three weeks
later, 2,000 miles away in Boise, Idaho, with $1.65 in his
pocket.

School had been the source of arguments between Tommy
and his father from the time he was twelve. His grades were
horrendous, and Manville, Sr., apparently considered his
son's inability to attain a measure of scholastic achievement
a reflection on himself and his ability to raise the boy.

Tommy regarded his father as a larger-than-life Simon
Legree. This attitude on the part of both, carried on in later
years, resulted in periods of hatred, during which the elder
Manville would disinherit his son. When the hatred phase
passed Tommy would be reinherited. Luckily, when his father
died on October 24, 1925, Tommy was in a good-grace period,
and he was left ten million of the twenty-three-million-
dollar estate. He utilized the money to launch expensive ships
on the stormy sea of matrimony.

Tommy was seventeen when he first met Florence Huber, a twenty-one-year-old chorus girl, under the marquee of Wallack's Theater on Broadway and 46th Street. It was raining, and conversation was not hard to start. "It's really pouring, isn't it?" may not have been the most profound of observations, but it seemed a likely opening line, and young Manville recalled years later that he actually used it.

Before the evening ended he was in Florence's apartment. Tommy lost little time presenting the rest of his line, not the least of which was that he was the son of the multi-millionaire head of the largest asbestos company in the world. Florence was duly impressed with his credentials, and two days later they were married. Tommy had begun his marital odyssey.

Manville, Sr., was aboard the Cunard line *Berengaria*, returning from Paris, when he was informed of Tommy's marriage. Samuel Carter, a business associate of Manville's, said, "I never saw a more angry man than Manville when he received the wireless about Tommy's marriage."

After the ship docked Manville stormed into the Pier 16 office of the Cunard Line and telephoned his lawyer to change his will and "disinherit that son-of-a-bitch son of mine." This was the first of a series of disinheritances used by the irate father to vent his spleen on a completely unconcerned son.

When Tommy saw his father that evening, the result was an unmitigated disaster. As Tommy related it later, "My father called me every vile name under the sun. He said I was a son of a bitch of the first order, a disgrace to him and to the family, and that he never wanted to see me again. He told me to get the hell out and never come back.

"He was yelling that he would have the marriage annulled. He was bellowing so much I was getting worried, and when he went near the fireplace and the andirons I really got scared. So I decided I had better get out quick, and I opened the door to beat it, and the butler fell into the room. You should have seen the surprised look on his face. He was leaning against the door, listening. When I opened the door he just fell in. But he was wasting his time against that door. From the way my father was yelling he could have stood in the next block and heard everything."

Tommy took the annulment threat seriously and decided to trek to Maryland to go through the marriage ceremony again to be on the safe side. On arriving, he discovered that Maryland had an age requirement of eighteen for marriage without the consent of parents. The couple went to New Jersey, and the knot was tied again.

Now the problem of money arose. Heir-to-millions Tommy had fourteen dollars, and Florence had eighty-two dollars. Tommy could undoubtedly have borrowed from friends, he later said, but "It never occurred to me, and I wouldn't have done it anyway." Tommy decided to get a job.

Finding one, however, wasn't easy. The country was in the midst of a periodic recession, and Manville decided that the easiest place to get a job was—where else?—in one of his father's plants.

He applied to the employment office, giving his name. The employment manager, half in jest, asked whether he was related to the president of the company. He almost fell off his chair when Tommy answered, "Yes, he's my father."

In a quandary, the manager, James Connors, telephoned Manville, Sr., to apprise him of the situation and request instructions. Mr. Manville had left on a business trip to California. Manville's executive assistant, hesitant to make a decision in the matter, told Connors to hire Tommy until Mr. Manville returned. Tommy was hired as a laborer in the plant, for fifteen dollars a week.

Manville, Sr., returned two weeks later. Told what had

taken place he angrily called the plant manager and screamed, "Fire him. Today!"

An unhappy Manville, Jr., joined the ranks of the unemployed.

By this time Tommy and Florence were genuine friends as well as lovers. Florence had undoubtedly been motivated to marry Tommy by the Manville millions, but she had grown to like him. He was boyish, unaffected, and utterly lacking in pretense. The fact that he was now disinherited did not greatly disturb her. She realized that although Tommy was in the doghouse today, that state of affairs could easily change. She made every effort to make life pleasant, and "We decided to really make a go of it."

Tommy landed himself another job, this time as a bellhop in the plush old Waldorf-Astoria Hotel, then at Fifth Avenue and 34th Street. This job was abruptly terminated after three weeks when the manager of the hotel rang for Tommy to pick up two valises. He picked up the bags as an astonished Manville, Sr., looked on with a ludicrously open mouth, his face filled with utter disbelief.

Tommy was unemployed again twenty minutes later.

Dejected, he walked to his three-room third-floor flat at Third Avenue and 65th Street. The shimmering heat-haze of a muggy day made walking on the hot pavements a torture, but to save a nickel carfare the future heir to millions walked thirty-one blistering blocks.

The dingy building Tommy called home was no worse than others on the garbage-strewn block, all owned by a friend of Andrew Carnegie, who was then crusading for better living conditions for the poor. Carnegie could well have started the crusade with his friend Peter Collins, but that might have ended their friendship. The block was in one of the worst slum areas of the city.

Tommy's flat was hardly the most desirable in the building. The Third Avenue elevated trains screeched and rumbled by fourteen feet from his windows. Tommy and Florence had grown accustomed to it. They had also grown accustomed to cockroaches swarming all over their rooms. As Florence, not without a sense of humor, said, "It sometimes seemed they were playing tag, and sometimes it looked as if they were just out for exercise."

What did bother the newlyweds was walking up three flights of stairs filled with nauseating odors of decaying garbage. But the rent was only five dollars a month, and that was of prime importance.

On the day Tommy was fired from the Waldorf, Florence arrived from the corner A & P minutes after he came home. After he gloomily related what had happened, Florence burst into howls of laughter. Her eyes streaming, she said, "Can you imagine what he thought when he saw you in that monkey uniform picking up those bags?"

Florence realized, however, that it might be a while before there was a reconciliation between Manville and his son and she decided it would be necessary for her to return to dancing in a chorus. The next day she landed a job in a Broadway show.

Tommy was in the dumps. He had no profession or skills, and "For the first time in my life I realized the importance of an education." He was too stubborn to make overtures to his father and shocked at the thought of being supported by a wife.

He decided to go to a friend of the family, William S. Cooney, a Wall Street broker, and asked him for work, offering to do anything. Cooney gave him a job doing the only thing Tommy could do for him—driving a car. Manville became Cooney's chauffeur, and the job lasted a little more than a year.

During this period Tommy never heard from his father and made no attempt to get in touch with him. Florence made every effort to keep the marriage alive, but Tommy became morose. He later related, "Without realizing it we began to drift apart, and it was really my fault. After all, it takes two to tango."

Things really drifted, and neither made any effort to stop the drift. Tommy later said, "It is really vague in my mind as to what I did in the next two years or what she did. All I know is that the ballgame was over, and we finally separated in 1917."

The United States entered World War I on April 6, 1917, and Tommy was called in the draft but rejected for military duty because of physical disabilities. At about this time, Manville, Sr., without formally reconciling with his son, gave him a monthly allowance. Whether this was because the prodigal was separated from the wife the father had so strongly opposed, or whether the sight of so many young men going off to war touched his emotions about his only son, was something Manville, Sr., never discussed. But Tommy's monetary difficulties were over.

Although now financially emancipated, he made no effort to resume relations with Florence; in fact, "I didn't even know where she was, and I just didn't care."

Tommy was begining to enjoy life, and at this point he inaugurated his playboy career. Wartime nightlife in New York was filled with brownouts, but nightclubs were teeming with frantic exuberance, the "live today, who knows what'll happen tomorrow?" attitude that comes only to a country at war. Thousands of young soldiers were on leave, trying to compress 120 minutes of living into every hour of life. And Tommy, though not in uniform, was trying to do the same.

The war dragged on, but on November 11, 1918, Armistice! Manville, Jr., would never forget that day.

The armistice was to be signed at eleven in the morning, and at exactly that minute pandemonium exploded throughout New York. The city was a madhouse. People surged and congregated everywhere, but especially in vast throngs milling on Fifth Avenue, on Broadway, in Times Square, and in the Wall Street area.

Tommy happened to be in front of the New York Stock Exchange. Ticker tape was being thrown from every window in the financial district, and it resembled a blizzard. Whistles blew. Horns blared. People were dancing in the streets, and total strangers were hugging each other.

Thousands were thronged in front of the statue of George Washington on the steps of the Sub-Treasury building, directly across from the J. P. Morgan bank at Broad and Wall Street. A group in front of the statue began singing "Over There." Before the song was half over, more than a hundred thousand people visible in the seven-block area joined in the singing. The volume was unbelievable, and when the crowd reached the words, "And we won't come back till it's over Over There," voices were breaking. Bankers, brokers, secretarys, and clerks—men and women of all ages and walks of life—were crying unashamedly. The war was over and fathers, sons, brothers, and sweethearts would be coming home.

But Tommy would be spending very little time at home. He now began to lead the complete night life, crawling home at five or six in the morning and sleeping all day. Finally, in November 1921, his father issued an ultimatum: "I'll discontinue your damn allowance until you change your ways." Manville would then sermonize his son endlessly on the twin blessings of hard work and clean living.

For Tommy it was wasted sanctimony. However, deciding

that it would be wise not to irritate his sole source of income, he resolved to go along in the hope that a short attendance at his father's office would be sufficient "to satisfy the old man" and gradually enable him to reembrace his old ways.

For the next three months Tommy showed up at the Johns-Manville executive offices daily and dutifully sat in on meetings and conferences. As he later said, "It was enough to last a lifetime. I saw company officials sitting around at the meetings, all nodding their heads and wagging their tongues when my father gave his thoughts on a subject, and I decided to do the same. It worked great. I agreed with anything and everything he said, and he really began to think of me as a coming executive. He soon thought I was working too hard and suggested I take a few weeks' vacation. I took six months, and nobody ever knew the difference, and my father didn't seem to care."

Tommy had underestimated his father, who was worrying plenty about his only son. As he remarked to a friend, "Insanity is hereditary. Parents get it from their children." Junior's actions weren't driving him crazy, but they were giving him sleepless nights.

Tommy was now thirty-one, but it was not yet apparent that he would become the country's "career bridegroom." The later public image of Manville, Jr., as one who seemed to be taking a new bride every year seemed remote as a rocket flight to the moon when Tommy celebrated his thirty-first birthday. (Florence Huber had obtained an uncontested divorce in Pennsylvania on April 12, 1922, on the grounds of desertion. At the time no money settlement was made, but after Tommy acquired his inheritance he gave her over one hundred thousand dollars.)

Now the elder Manville's thoughts regarding his son and marriage took a 180-degree turn. He hoped that Tommy would settle down and continue the Manville name.

Tommy, however, had other ideas and apparently didn't have the faintest intention of entering into any further bonds of matrimony. Despite his millions, Manville couldn't force his stubborn son to get married. It was circumstances, and the Johns-Manville corporate offices, that solved the problem.

Manville told his son that the company was about to embark on a new corporate program and that he wanted Tommy to attend the initial meetings. Feeling that a few weeks' attendance would be followed by another six-month vacation, Tommy raised no objections. He arrived at the office the day after Labor Day, 1925. It was a memorable day.

A meeting had been set for eleven in the morning, and Tommy was in his father's office promptly at ten-thirty. He felt the "old man" would appreciate that gesture. Manville began to go over the purpose of the meeting with his son and rang for his secretary to bring him a file. Into the office walked what Tommy later described as a "beautiful vision."

She was young, blonde, and beautiful, with "lusty jugs."

Lois Arline McCoin had been Manville, Sr.'s secretary for six months, and rumor in the office was that she was more than a secretary. This rumor never bothered Lois, for as she told Miriam Cooper, secretary to a vice-president, "Mr. Manville is a perfect gentleman. And besides, he wouldn't know what to do with it if I threw it at him."

Tommy's eyes were riveted on Lois, and Manville, Sr., not unaware of what was happening, saw a possible solution to the problem of matrimony for his son. Thereafter, on Tommy's visits to the office, his father would ring for files and have Tommy and Lois go over them, hoping that nature would take its course. It was much like a farmer baiting a fox to come into the henhouse.

On October 1, 1925, Tommy married Lois in the New York Municipal Building.

The happy couple traveled to Bermuda for a honeymoon, and as Tommy observed, "I really didn't realize I was married until the second night. I was having a drink at the bar with a girl, and Lois walked up and reminded me. I didn't like being reminded, and maybe I used some strong language in telling her. Lois checked out to go to another hotel. I wouldn't let the bellboy take her bags, and after yelling and screaming for an hour she finally agreed to stay. But I knew then the marriage wouldn't last—she was pulling the strings too tight."

The story Lois later told friends was a bit different. Her insight perhaps explained the inner workings of the Manville heir. "Tommy never enjoyed being married," she explained. "For him the fun was in the chase. When he caught what he was after, the game was over for him. I took exactly three days to realize it."

It took Tommy less than three days. He now made no effort to hide his lack of interest in poor Lois. This did not prevent practically every other male in the hotel from giving her the once-over twice; she was a stunning woman.

One week after Tommy and Lois returned from their honeymoon, Manville, Sr., died in the Plaza Hotel of an apparent heart attack.

Two weeks after Manville's death the newlyweds went to live in Tommy's apartment at 128 Central Park South. Lois, feeling that being married to a millionaire entitled *her* to live like one, went on a shopping spree. The bills were sent, of course, to Tommy. When he received them, a month later, he couldn't believe it—they totaled more than thirty-eight thousand dollars. He informed Lois, "The marriage is over—*kaput*—and I don't want you charging anything more." To make certain there was no misunderstanding he said he intended to put an advertisement in the newspapers that he wouldn't be responsible for her debts.

Feeling that Tommy was serious, Lois decided to make the rounds of a few stores before he had a chance to carry out his threat. She charged twenty-four thousand dollars' worth of clothes and furs at various establishments, and at Tiffany's she made purchases totaling nineteen thousand dollars. As she later said, "I felt I was entitled to going-away presents, and I gave myself some."

When Tommy received the new bills he exploded. In a fit of anger he threw a heavy bronze ashtray into a mirror, then grabbed a broomstick and smashed two oriental vases Lois had bought. "He ranted and raved for at least ten minutes," his maid later told the press. She had been cleaning up in the bedroom, and in the midst of her boss's tantrum she discreetly decided to take the rest of the day off.

Tommy went down to the *New York Times* that afternoon, and inserted the ad, to appear the day before Christmas: "Having left my bed and board I hereby notify the public that I am not responsible in any way for debts or actions of any nature incurred by Mrs. T. F. Manville, Jr." Tommy told friends, *"That* is Lois's Christmas gift."

However, since Lois had purchased her going-away presents before the notice appeared, Tommy was legally bound to pay for them. Surprisingly, he held no animosity toward her for doing what she had. He said, "I really don't blame her. She felt she deserved them, and maybe she did. But I had to do what I did, because at the rate she was going ten million dollars wasn't going to last too long."

They separated, and this seemed to buoy Tommy's spirits. He now evinced that peculiar trait which he displayed with every one of his wives—once they no longer lived together he had the friendliest of feelings toward them and they enjoyed the most cordial relations.

Lois finally went off to Reno to untie the strings. She happily joined the divorce colony that was then the mainstay of the Reno economy and spent an agreeable three months, which Nevada law required to establish residency to break the marital bonds. When the hotel would not permit her to keep a pet wire-haired terrier on the premises, she solved that problem by moving out and renting a large, expensive house, through the courtesy of her accommodating about-to-be-ex, Tommy.

The uncontested divorce was granted on the grounds of desertion. Tommy settled forty thousand dollars a year on Lois. In all, Tommy was to wind up paying $1,870,000 to his eleven wives. It was obviously worthwhile and highly profitable to become a Manville ex-wife.

On May 21, 1931, Tommy was back in the Municipal Building to say "I do." This time, it was the "real thing." Manville watchers, of whom there were now many, had no trouble picking out the bride. She was young, blonde, busty, and beautiful. Avonne Taylor was a former Follies chorus girl who, like Tommy, had been married twice before. For her, too, this was to be the "real thing."

Tommy's friends were betting among themselves that the marriage would last two months. Jimmy Walker, then Mayor of New York and a steady nightclub pal of Tommy's, said, "Tommy's marriage attention span is one week. I'll bet it doesn't last two weeks." Babe Ruth, a good friend of Tommy's, gave it one month, and his guess was closest. Marital bliss lasted thirty-four days; then the Manvilles separated.

On November 24, 1931, Mrs. Avonne Taylor Manville arrived in Campeche, Mexico to secure the divorce. Tommy was a bachelor again. The settlement was rumored at two hundred thousand dollars but was never disclosed except in jest by Tommy, who figured it had cost him "about six thousand dollars per night."

Jimmy Walker, noted for his wit, observed, "Tommy is calculating the sum according to the calendar days. If you figure it out by what most likely happened, it is two hundred thousand dollars for *one night*. Period. That's what I call nice work, if you can get it."

By now news of Manville's lavish marital expenditures was continually in gossip columns and the purported two-hundred-thousand-dollar settlement jarred many people. This was at the height of the Great Depression, when hundreds of thousands of people in large cities were struggling to earn a few dollars a day selling apples on street corners. Millions were out of work. "Brother, Can You Spare a Dime?" was the nation's theme song. Money was short, breadlines were long, people were desperate. The well-publicized tossing around of huge sums by Tommy on frivolity apparently stirred anger in many, who began to write anonymous letters threatening bodily harm to Manville for his profligate ways.

Manville enjoyed making news. Unlike some of his wealthy contemporaries, whose lives were equally incredible but whose advisors employed expensive public-relations experts to keep their adventures out of the press, Manville couldn't have cared less.

But Tommy made the mistake of telling a newspaper friend of the threatening mail he was being sent. The publication by the news media that Manville was receiving such letters turned a relative trickle into a flood, and threats were made that alarmed the multimillionaire. His friend Mayor Jimmy Walker (who would have to resign in 1932 to prevent his removal by Governor Franklin D. Roosevelt on grounds of corruption in city affairs) took the matter up with Police Commissioner Mulrooney.

It was highly unusual for a mayor to intervene at the highest police level in an essentially local police matter.

Ordinary John Q. Citizen, and even some of minor importance, in a similar situation would be told to take the matter up with the postal authorities or the local police precinct, which in all probability would advise him to be careful and let it go at that.

But Jimmy Walker was never one to let a pal down, especially one who frequently picked up the nightclub tabs for His Honor and guests. To protect the golden goose, Mayor Walker ordered the police commissioner to assign detectives of the East 51st Street Station to guard Tommy until the storm blew over.

The police protection caused Tommy to be circumspect for a while, but in a month he was back in circulation. He was not especially concerned about the public brouhaha regarding his extravagance. "After all," he said, "I didn't cause this depression. Why don't they write their bitching letters to Herbert Hoover?"

The police protection would have been useful one week after it was discontinued. Tommy was accosted outside a nightclub by a beefy drunk who was looking for a fight and happened to bump into Manville. "Why don't you look where you're going, you stupid bastard?" he said. "I ought to spit in your eye." The language was vile, the act was repulsive, but the aim was true. Right in the eye!

By this time—1932—Tommy had decided the purpose of life—his life— was *living,* and he intended and could afford to do just that. He acquired a twenty-eight-room mansion on Premium Point in New Rochelle. Five magnificent acres reached from the mainland through a privately policed area.

He equipped the house and grounds with burglar alarms, peephole doors, armed guards, a public-address system, a forty-seat movie theater, radios in every room, and twenty telephones. He looked on the estate as his fortress against "nuts" and often ambled around the premises with two heavy pistols in his belt.

Tommy named the house Bon Repos (Good Rest) but later re-christened it Bon Brawl. His friends frequently referred to it as the Observation Ward. The estate bordered on Long Island Sound, and Tommy purchased a yacht, which he named *No*. He said the name fooled no one, since the answer was usually yes.

How could a Manville home be complete without a wife? On October 9, 1933, the owner of the Observation Ward, having once more found a young woman to meet his specifications, married Marcelle Edwards. He had discovered his new dream in the Earl Carroll Vanities instead of the Ziegfeld Follies. When Tommy proposed, Marcelle quickly accepted. Since she was only twenty, her mother's written consent was required. It was swiftly and happily supplied.

The ceremony took place at the Pickwick Arms, in Greenwich, Connecticut, and the yacht *No* transported the guests to the Manville estate at Premium Point for a reception. Tommy set a record for the trip: "I quarreled with no one!"

However, he soon quarreled with Marcelle, and the newlyweds were separated in April 1934. There was a slight change of pace—to everyone's surprise there was a reconciliation in June instead of the expected divorce.

But on August 6, 1935, Marcelle began divorce proceedings in the New York Supreme Court. Charging cruelty and abandonment, she alleged in her complaint that Manville "wounded her sensibilities by violent language and on several occasions had used her roughly, striking her on June 20." She further alleged that when he sailed for Europe on June 22 he engaged accommodations for two other women.

Talking with friends about Marcelle's allegations, Tommy laughed that he had never used language she hadn't heard before and that "this business of engaging accommodations for two other women was not correct. It was for three women."

But an unexpected development was hovering in the wings. Marcelle withdrew her complaint when Manville returned from Europe. The "newlyweds" were back in Bon Repos, which soon again turned into Bon Brawl. Within two days Tommy was calling on the New Rochelle Police Department to "send police and an ambulance to remove my wife!"

Why he requested an ambulance was a complete mystery. Had anyone been hurt? The ambulance doctor flatly refused to become involved. The police decided to be prudent and have a policeman remain the house the rest of the night "to keep the peace."

Tommy confided to Winchell, "Walter, it is now Round 24 of a never-ending fight." Finally fed up, he moved to solve his problem via the usual divorce-and-cash-settlement route.

The minute his decision was made known, Tommy and Marcelle were again the best of friends. He saw her off on the flight from Newark to Reno and presented her with a bouquet of orchids. To demonstrate that Tommy was "orchids" with her, Marcelle was cradling them when she got off the plane. Her settlement was reported to be two hundred thousand dollars. When Tommy was asked to confirm that it was in that neighborhood, he said, "That's what I call a nice neighborhood!"

After the divorce from wife number four, Tommy resolved, "Never again!"

He returned to the nightclub scene but found it somewhat boring and preferred private entertainment at home. Soon the parties he hosted at Bon Repos were rumored to be considerably livelier than any shows in public night spots, and there was quite a scramble among celebrities to receive invitations.

As the reputation of the soirees spread, disgruntled persons who were not on Tommy's invitation list were sour-graping by remarking, "Bon Repos is the biggest whorehouse in Westchester." This, of course, was grist for hungry gossip mills and only added to the desirability of the elusive invitation.

Asked about the parties, Jimmy Walker, now ex-mayor of New York and an infrequent guest at Bon Repos, said, "If all the girls at Tommy's parties were laid end to end I wouldn't be a bit surprised."

Tommy decided to make architectural changes at Bon Repos. Since alterations would be extensive, he moved into a suite at New York's Astor Hotel. It was a short stroll from the hotel to New York night life, and he was welcomed back like a returning hero.

The red carpet was out for him everywhere. He was again the big-time spender. His varied nightclub companions ranged from politicians, theatrical personages, and athletes to mobsters and racketeers.

Manville's lawyer, Mark Eisner, was a law partner of ex-Judge George W. Olvany, who had been a leader of Tammany Hall. Disturbed at stories he heard about some of Tommy's companions, he remonstrated with him about his choice of friends.

"You really ought to be careful associating with known mobsters and racketeers" he told him. "People will talk, and it won't do your reputation any good."

Eisner wasn't the first who had brought the matter up, and Tommy had always laughed it off. On the morning Eisner offered his advice, Manville had had a tooth extracted, and apparently Eisener had picked the wrong day to berate his client. Ordinarily Tommy would have again laughed, but today he let loose with an unexpected and unusual verbal torrent.

"Listen, Mark, I've also been associating with a lot of political leaders, and you're not warning me against them, are you? And there aren't a bigger bunch of thieves and hypocrites in the country. They're worse than racketeers. They're a bunch of grafting, crooked, lying sons-of-bitches who hold themselves out to be honest people."

Eisner was aghast. "Are you saying I'm a grafting, crooked, lying son of a bitch?"

"Wait a minute, Mark. Wait a minute. I didn't say that. I think you're not. I really do. And that's just the point. The fact that you associate with the bastards doesn't make you one. But haven't you read about all the political corruption the Seabury investigation brought out? There aren't a more corrupt bunch of bastards in the country than political bosses. Let's stop the bullshit, Mark, and stop worrying about my friends. You had better start worrying about yours."

Eisner was surprised and shocked. He had never dreamed that Tommy had thoughts on matters political or that he had done anything but glance at newspapers during the sensational Seabury investigation of corruption in city affairs.

But Tommy had a particular interest in this scandal because it involved his close friend Jimmy Walker. Manville blamed Walker's forced resignation as mayor of New York on the actions of the political bosses who controlled Tammany Hall. From either Walker or close associates, Tommy had received the distinct impression that Walker had been made a scapegoat and patsy for the corruption of powerful political leaders.

Tommy had enjoyed the wit and company of Walker and now really missed him. His association with the mayor had put him close to the trappings of power, and he enjoyed basking in the glory of being an intimate friend of the head of City Hall. Walker's departure from the seats of the mighty was a big blow.

Eisner was angered at what Tommy was saying and at the tone of his voice. "Are you telling me that men like La Guardia and Tom Dewey are corrupt politicians?" (La Guardia was then mayor of New York City, and Dewey was District Attorney of New York County.)

"What the hell are you talking about?" countered Tommy. "I didn't say that. They're not corrupt, but that's because they don't have political bosses controlling them."

"Well, who are you talking about?" asked Eisner.

"I'm talking about the political bosses, the sons-of-bitches that control political power in New York," retorted Manville angrily. "You're talking about office holders, and most of them would be honest if the bosses would let them. I'm talking about bosses who are political pimps, who prostitute public officials into doing what they shouldn't do and turn office holders into political whores."

"Are you telling me there are no bosses who aren't what you call 'political pimps'?"

"Well," answered Tommy, "I'd say the chances of finding a political boss who isn't is about the same as finding a virgin whore."

Three days later Tommy had a new lawyer.

Tommy continued in blissful bachelorhood until November 18, 1941. As his fifth bride, he took Bonita Edwards. This was somewhat confusing, since the last name of his fourth bride was also Edwards, and many thought he had remarried Marcelle. Others thought it was Marcelle's sister. But Bonita was someone entirely new.

She was a twenty-two-year-old Follies girl, "with headlights you can see from forty paces." The marriage took place at the Silvermine Tavern in Norwalk, Connecticut.

Tommy was now forty-seven and looked sixty. His hair was completely gray, and although he considered it distinguished and took pride in it, his aging appearance didn't exactly conform to the image of Manville as a youthful lover that was being projected by columnists. Mark Hellinger observed, "I don't know why the hell he got married again. The guy can hardly crawl into bed."

Tommy didn't crawl for long. Seventeen days later Bonita arrived in Reno to establish residence for a divorce. The grounds: irreconcilable differences. She was accompanied by her mother, which made for an appealing picture of Bonita in the newspapers.

Bonita's complaint was that Manville "treated her with extreme cruelty, entirely mental in character, which caused her great unhappiness and injured her general health." However, it did not injure her financial health, since Miss Edwards registered no complaint about the amount of the settlement.

World War II began for the United States on December 7, 1941, when the Japanese attacked Pearl Harbor. The war naturally reduced the coverage of Tommy in the newspapers somewhat, but during this time of national crisis his shenanigans, though personal and harming no one but himself, angered and offended many people. Derogatory Manville "Letters to the Editor" poured in. A few of the more unprintable missives found their way into the newsrooms, where they circulated, and the consensus of the writers seemed to be that Tommy was a "first-class horse's ass."

Actually, Tommy was not doing much that was newsworthy. Then, on October 11, 1942, he married Wilhelmina Connelly Boze, a twenty-year-old actress, better know as "Billy."

Billy naturally filled the Manville specifications, and then some. She was a sultry beauty, a young Southern woman from Andrews, South Carolina.

For a change of pace Manville had this wedding performed in the New Rochelle City Hall, and after the ceremony the principals and guests returned to the groom's home on Premium Point, where the ceremony was repeated. For sentimental reasons, a recording was made of the ceremony.

"This is one wedding I can't understand," said Al Jolson, hearing the news on the radio while enroute to New York with two pals, both Broadway columnists. "I know Billy, and I know she isn't out for Tommy's money. With her looks and brains she could get the cream of the crop instead of the cream of the crap. Why she's doing it I don't know. It won't last a month."

Jolson was wrong. The marriage lasted two months, and Billy was in Reno in February to untie the knot. But there was a surprise in this divorce. Jolson was right that Billy was not after Tommy's money, for she insisted on an agreement that there would be no alimony, support, or maintenance. This news was greeted by astonished "wait and see's" by café society sophisticates.

Billy arrived for her Reno-vation wearing the Manville emblem—six orchids to denote that she was the sixth wife of the multimillionaire whom many now considered to have "some weird sex hangup." Was Tommy into sado-masochism? Did he go for off-beat sex? Did he chain his wives to the bed and slap their behinds? Did he want sex fourteen different ways, including hanging from the chandelier? Was he for real?

The puzzle was why Billy had married Manville in the first place and why she divorced him if it wasn't for the money. Romantic young writers of magazine articles gushed that it was because she really loved him, but wiser

writers asked: "What is there to love about Tommy Manville except his money?"

The only reason Billy offered for calling it a day was that
Tommy had become very agitated, almost hysterical, over the
length of time she took in ordering dinner at a New York
restaurant. This sounded absurd, but it was as good as any
of the other reasons for a Manville divorce. Perhaps better.

But Billy swore it was true. To add to the confusion, the
day after the divorce she took the first plane for New York to
meet Tommy for dinner.

Tommy had now made six trips to the altar, and he decided
to "put it on canvas" for posterity. He commissioned a well-
known artist to paint larger-than-life portraits of his six wives,
to be hung in the hallway at Bon Repos. Dapper actor
Adolph Menjou, a good friend of Tommy's, recalled that
after the paintings were in place Tommy would stand in
front of a particular one for five or ten minutes, and just
stare.

Menjou once spoke while Tommy was staring, and Tommy,
in a quiet but tense tone, said, "Please, Adolph—never interrupt me when I'm looking at my wife."

"Tommy would never stare at more than one picture in any
one day," Menjou said. "In that way apparently Tommy was
true to the wife of that day."

Macie Marie ("Sunny") Ainsworth had been married four
times before she was twenty years old! This was to be her
fifth wedding. It was Tommy's seventh. Tommy, who appeared to be nervous as an amateur hearing wedding bells
for the first time, before the ceremony whispered to his soon-
to-be wife, "This is your last chance to walk out. Do you want
to run?" Sunny had no such intention. Obviously, her mother
hadn't raised a stupid child.

They were married in the Supreme-Court chambers of Justice Valente, who had known Tommy for a long time. The date was August 25, 1943, less than six months since the termination of his marriage to Billy Boze. In a little less than eight hours, Sunny and Tommy were separated. Eight hours!

Friends of Tommy's, schmoozing at Lindy's that night, seriously considered having a guardian appointed for him. His action seemed incomprehensible. What was the point of it? Was he mentally sick? They had been married at eleven in the morning, and by seven in the evening it was all over.

Jimmy Braddock, former heavyweight champion, walked into Lindy's while a noisy and boisterous discussion was going on. Asked what he thought about Tommy and the eight-hour marriage, Braddock replied, "The guy's punch drunk. He's been hit in the balls too often."

Crazy or not, Tommy and Sunny had been legally wed, and she was off to Reno to collect her pay. She received seventy-five thousand dollars; for eight hours, it came to a far higher wage than she received in the chorus.

This marriage resulted in another flood of derogatory mail: "Put your money to better use!" Some letters were from women who offered him cheaper rates. And men wrote that they would make him happy at a fraction of the cost. One Idaho farmer wrote, "My brother is in a mental institution. They ought to let him out and put you in."

"Never again!" said Tommy. He went back to intense partying. His parties were still riotous affairs, but his eagerness to bet anyone any amount that he would never marry again convinced some optimists that he had really made up his mind. Was it remotely possible that Tommy had finally grown up?

In December 1945, a friend of Tommy's, Charles Townley,

met Winchell and told him, "Walter, I think Tommy's going to dive in again. She's a British girl."

Winchell ran an item, mentioning only that "it looks like Tommy Manville is going to the cleaners again."

Tommy phoned him, upset, and said, "Walter, you were never more wrong. I told you, 'Never again!' "

"Never again" took place in Larchmont on December 13, 1945. The bride was Georgina Campbell, a twenty-seven-year-old English woman. Although she was a writer and not in show business, she fitted the Manville measurements perfectly. They had met at a Bon Repos party when she was on assignment to interview Tommy for the *Hobo News*, a well-known off-beat paper of the day.

In the interview she had asked him, "Mr. Manville, does money bring you happiness?"

"Well," said Tommy, "money may not bring happiness, but it certainly permits a person to enjoy misery in comfort."

Georgina thought that was quite clever. "You are a man of great wealth, and people undoubtedly tend to flatter you. Do you believe the flattering things they tell you?"

Tommy now became profound. "Flattery," he said, "is like a perfume. It is pleasant to inhale but dangerous to swallow."

Her final question was, "Mr. Manville, why have you turned down invitations to join two of the most prestigious clubs in Westchester?"

Tommy answered, "I wouldn't want to belong to a club that would have me for a member."

"How could you not love a man like that?" asked Georgina.

Tommy liked quite a few things about Georgina. He liked her charming English accent and a few other, visible charms. They saw each other, on and off, for six months. Tommy continually told her, "I'm not going to get married again. I mean it."

Georgina didn't argue. "Of course you do, and it's a wise decision."

On December 13th they were married.

In statements to the press after the wedding, Tommy evidently felt her background needed some glamorizing. He described her as an assistant New York correspondent for the *London Daily Mirror* and a Hollywood correspondent for the *London Daily Mail*.

Tommy Manville was now a household name throughout the country. Everywhere he went in public, the curious collected. In theaters people turned around and gawked if Tommy was present. One evening, on the stage at the Winter Garden, Milton Berle said, "We have several celebrities here tonight. Is that Tommy Manville sitting in the tenth row with his fourth wife or in the fourth row with his tenth wife?" Actually it was Tommy in the sixth row with his eighth wife, Georgina.

This marriage followed the familiar Manville pattern. It endured five weeks; then Georgina was off for Reno.

But now came a change in the script. Georgina returned from Reno with the announcement, "I'm not going to get a divorce." Apparently she had received legal advice that it would be more profitable to remain married than be an ex-wife. She bluntly informed Tommy that she would never divorce him, no matter what.

Tommy was nonplussed. The situation had never arisen before. It upset him.

Being on excellent terms with all of his former wives, he decided to have lunch with number four, Marcelle Edwards, to discuss the situation and ask her advice. Since she had previously been in a similar situation, what did she think Georgina had in mind? Halfway through lunch Marcelle came up with a simple solution: "Take it up with your lawyer."

Tommy's lawyers found the situation something they had

hoped for for a long time. Since Georgina did not seem to mind being married and separated, it was decided that to protect Tommy from getting married again, it would be best for him to stay in the position that seemed so agreeable to Georgina.

In that way no one could have their hooks out to marry Tommy. For that matter, Tommy would be in no position to fish in blonde and busty seas, for it seemed that when Tommy went fishing, he always managed to get caught by the fish.

This solution appealed to Manville as "marriage insurance." A happy Georgina agreed to a legal separation under an agreement by which Tommy paid her a thousand dollars a month. "The thousand dollars a month is to stay away from me," Tommy explained.

The arrangement seemed to suit them both, but far from making her "stay away from me," Tommy invited her to lunch two or three times a week. She frequently drove to Bon Repos to have lunch or breakfast.

While Georgina was driving up to meet him one morning, her car was in a collision near White Plains and she was killed.

Georgina had indeed been "marriage insurance" for Tommy. He was married to her from 1945 to 1952. Only three months after her death, he was married again.

"He's crazy and ought to be in a nuthouse!" was the mildest of the comments at Lindy's when Tommy took his ninth wife, Anita Frances Roddy-Eden, on July 10, 1952.

She was an exotic-looking twenty-nine-year-old songwriter, and the ceremony was performed in the New Rochelle City Hall by the mayor, Stanley Church.

The marriage caused waves of excitement and a flood in the City Hall. When word got around that Tommy Manville and his ninth bride were in the building everyone stepped into the hall to catch a glimpse. The crowd, speaking in low but excited tones, included a plumber who had been fixing a main pipe in the men's toilet. He had sent his assistant to the basement to turn on a valve to test the water pressure, when the Manville commotion brought him out into the hall. He went to the front of the hall and craned his neck like everyone else and waited to catch a glimpse, forgetting about the open valve in the toilet. He was joltingly reminded of it when his excited assistant shouted, "Charley, Charley, where are you? There's a flood in the hall!"

One of the Westchester newspapers headlined the story, "Manville Wedding Causes Flood in Men's Toilet!"

In Lindy's the next day, one of the waiters asked Leo Lindy, "You mean they held the ceremony in the toilet? Boy, what an idea for a wedding!"

Two weeks later Anita was getting a Mexican divorce in Reynosa, a border town near McAllen, Texas. The Manville checkbook showed a hundred-thousand-dollar entry as money accepted by Anita in lieu of alimony.

Tommy was now fifty-eight. Bon Repos was booming, with parties almost every night, but it was all becoming a bore to Tommy. He was tired. After a quiet 1955 New Year's Eve celebration, there were no more parties. He decided to sell Bon Repos, and it was purchased by William Black, millionaire head of Chock Full O'Nuts.

The old Manville flair was petering out. It was five years before he married again. He was sixty-three, and anyone guessing his age would have said eighty. His bride, Patricia Gaston, was a Texas chorus girl, six inches taller and twenty-seven years younger than Tommy.

On May 5, 1957, they were married in New York's plush Hotel Pierre by Judge Mitchell Schweitzer (who was later to resign from the Supreme Court to prevent a trial to remove him for corrupt conduct).

This marriage wasn't expected to last, and Tommy didn't disappoint his friends. Patricia dutifully reported to Reno, set up the necessary residence, and was awarded a divorce on the grounds of mental cruelty. There was a sealed agreement covering the amount of the settlement and the property rights, but it was rumored to be two hundred thousand dollars.

At sixty-six Tommy did it again. It was his last hurrah. The date was January 12, 1960. This time, however, the scenario contained an interesting twist.

Christina Erdlen was a waitress at the North Court Restaurant in White Plains. One day Tommy and his lawyer went there for lunch, after an appearance in the County Courthouse involving some Manville property. Tommy wound up with more than lunch.

Tommy was fascinated with Christina when she came to take their order. "A living doll!" he told his lawyer.

Although it was the first time Tommy had ever seen her, he knew "she was the girl of my dreams." But by the time Tommy reached the coffee and cake he knew he had a problem.

Usually when Tommy was as fascinated as he was with Christina he would get married within a few days, "before the fascination wore off." He was prepared to follow that custom and take his eleventh wife, but there was a slight hitch. Christina was already married, to a barber who worked a few doors away.

Not one to let the small matter of her being married to

someone else stand in the way of true love, Tommy had a solution—arrange for Christina to obtain a quickie Mexican divorce.

Wedding bells chimed for Tommy and Christina on January 12, 1960. The marriage lasted until October 9, 1967.

On that day bells again rang for Tommy. Not wedding bells. Tommy Manville was dead.

Anger? Recrimination? Revenge? That was never Tommy's philosophy of marriage and divorce. "I loved them when I married them, and the fact we were divorced did not really change my feelings for them."

The logic of this philosophy escaped many people, because it did not conform to normal experience. But in matters of marriage Tommy was spectacularly nonconformist. A "normal" standard of behavior was hardly the yardstick by which to measure him.

His incredible peccadilloes had cost him almost three million dollars in marriage settlements and legal fees. Had Manville any regrets? "Every penny was well spent," he said to Ed Sullivan. "I know some of the biggest men in the country who spent a lot more on hobbies and ended up with a lot less."

Many people, including life-long friends, found his actions ridiculous, complex, and unexplainable. Perhaps Lois, his second wife, came closest to the answer: "For Tommy, the fun was in the chase."

Leonard "Kip" Rhinelander
versus
Alice Rhinelander

"Disrobe to the waist!"

The woman blanched, shooting an embarrassed glance at her audience. Then she began to undress.

This wasn't happening at the famed Minsky's burlesque in Manhattan—it was in the dignified County Court Building in White Plains, New York. A Justice of the Supreme Court of the State of New York had ordered the lady to disrobe in the juryroom. This was not a case of a jurist who was lecherous; it was a case of annulment. The purpose was to help a jury decide whether a blue-blood socialite had been fraudulently misled into marriage with a "Negress" who allegedly held herself out to be white.

The date was November 23, 1925.

Leonard "Kip" Rhinelander was a blue blood, according to the standards set by the *Social Register*. He stuttered and stammered, and was barely able to hold a conversation, but that carried little weight with those who decided who were the social elite. He was a scion of the Rhinelander family, whose vast real estate holdings went back to the days when

New York was a colony of England. That made Rhinelander a blue blood, regardless of what he looked like, how he acted, or how he sounded.

Rhinelander had committed the social sin of marrying a decidedly red-blooded, non-Caucasian female. Furthermore, the young woman in question, Alice Jones, came from a lower rung of the economic ladder. She was the daughter of a taxi-cab driver.

In the juryroom Alice's lawyers were trying to show that unless Leonard required a Seeing Eye dog, he must have known that Alice was not a candidate for admission to the Daughters of the American Revolution.

Rhinelander's lawyers were attempting to annul the marriage on the ground that their client had been duped into believing Alice to be white. Had Rhinelander known his beloved was "colored," he alleged, he would not have married her.

This was to be one of the most provocative, revealing, and sensational matrimonial cases in the history of the United States.

White America was both apathetic and shockingly indifferent to the rights of blacks in the 1920s. Militant Negroes were brutally squelched. In most Southern states and a few Northern ones, a black was defined as a person having "even one drop of Negro blood." The Ku Klux Klan was at its peak and had visibly demonstrated its strength by staging a forty thousand-man parade down Pennsylvania Avenue in Washington. Its national membership in 1925 had swelled to more than four million.

(Included in this number was a young man named Harry S. Truman, who in 1945 was to become President of the United States. He had joined the KKK in 1922, and as a matter of political expediency quietly resigned from the Klan before he was elected a member of the United States Senate from Missouri.)

At the time of the Rhinelander brouhaha, antimiscegenation statutes existed in many states. These statutes were held to be constitutional, since the Thirteenth and Fourteenth Amendments were construed as securing civil and political rights only, and not those of a social or domestic nature. The case of Plessy v. Ferguson, decided by the Supreme Court of the United States in 1896, put the legal stamp of approval on segregated facilities for the races.

There were whites who would gladly have welcomed the Negro as a brother in the brotherhood of Man, but there were few, very few, who would welcome him as a brother-in-law. Leonard Rhinelander's father decidedly was not one of them. He was predictably aghast at the marriage.

The Rhinelander case was a bombshell of spectacular proportions. It painfully revealed the deep-rooted prejudice that existed against mixed marriages, and against blacks.

When traveling in the South, blacks had to ride in the back of the bus or on Jim Crow trains. There were no exceptions. It made no difference whether the person was Booker T. Washington, the great educator, George Washington Carver, the internationally known scientist, a doctor, lawyer, college graduate with a Phi Beta Kappa key, cotton-picking field-hand, or a shoe-shine boy. They were all equally guilty of the crime of being "colored." And they all had to ride where they were told they belonged.

The South operated on the theory that the best way to compel compliance with restrictive laws was to make the penalty swift and sure. Southern courts were very co-operative. Constitutional rights for blacks were trampled on or completely ignored. The statue of Justice atop many a courthouse must have wept at what went on inside some of the courtrooms.

Prejudice was hardly confined to travel—or to the South. It applied to all phases of relationships between blacks and whites. In the North, East, and West, people had their own way of drawing color lines. It was a fact of national life in the 1920s. The "Roaring Twenties" did not do much roaring for the blacks.

Laws protecting Negroes in the North—that section of the country erroneously regarded as "the black man's haven"—worked fully as well as Prohibition laws then in effect. In-otherwords, nearly everyone ignored them.

For the most part the lowliest and most illiterate whites in the nation considered themselves superior to the wealthiest, most talented, or educated black. While one person couldn't necessarily tell whether another was an illiterate just by look-ing at him, one could tell a person was black. Unless he or she was so light that they could "pass," and conveniently forget their ancestry. There were tens of thousands who had "passed," and had left a legacy of puzzlement in many a white household when the birth of a child with Negroid features or hair caused bewildered glances and shaking of heads among relatives and friends.

Leonard "Kip" Rhinelander was born, on October 2, 1902, into a family that traced its American ancestry back to the late 1600s. Before 1700 the first Rhinelander had acquired large land holdings. In the early 1900s they were among the largest landowners in the country.

Leonard's father, Philip Rhinelander, was distinguished in manner and appearance, and his ancestry opened doors to "sacred membership" in prestigious historical societies con-fined to descendants of those who came to America before

1700. He was arrogant most of the time and overbearing the rest of the time. But by dint of his lineage and the sheer weight of his financial resources he was respected by the social aristocracy. Some of his peers held him in sycophantic veneration, which he accepted as a matter of course. At a dinner in his honor for his contributions to the Metropolitan Museum of Art, one of the guests turned to William Randolph Hearst and said, "Why can't Philip be more democratic like the rest of us?"

"In that case," said Hearst, "he wouldn't be Philip Rhinelander."

Leonard had two brothers, T. J. Oakley Rhinelander and Philip Rhinelander II, both of whom resembled their father. Leonard, however, favored his mother, Adeline, who died horribly when Leonard was fourteen, from burns suffered when a lamp exploded in the family mansion in Tuxedo Park, New York.

Leonard was a pleasant, quiet, unassuming young man. The background of events of his meeting Alice and their subsequent romance, marriage, separation, and trial read like a Hollywood script.

Leonard was plagued by stuttering and stammering from early boyhood, and in an effort to cure his speech defect, at the age of nineteen he was sent to a specialized school, the Orchard, at Shippan Point, Connecticut. While there he met Carl Kreitler, a young man his own age, who worked as an electrician at the school. They became friendly, and one day Leonard invited him and another acquaintance, John Boyd, to take a drive to test out his new car, a Stutz Bearcat.

The car stalled in New Rochelle, New York, and they pushed it to a gasoline station a short distance away. While they were joking and fixing the car, Grace Jones, a sister of Alice happened to pass by and stopped to watch. Grace was extremely pretty, and Carl struck up a conversation. It ended with the three boys taking Grace for a drive to Port Chester, New York.

Later, when the foursome arrived back in New Rochelle, Carl, who had taken a fancy to Grace, said to Leonard and Boyd, "Why don't you guys go to a diner and grab something to eat? I'm going to take Grace for a drive." Carl and Grace returned in an hour with happy expressions on their faces. The question "Where did you go?" went unanswered.

A few days later, as a favor to Carl, Leonard went back to New Rochelle to deliver a message to Grace at the service station where they had met her. While Leonard was delivering Carl's message, Grace's stunning sister Alice walked by, very obviously by prearrangement.

She walked with a slow, swinging step that set Leonard's thoughts racing and his pulse pounding. She had a wonderful figure. Alice was dark-complexioned, with huge, dark eyes and a smile that lit up her face. Leonard was particularly impressed by her dazzling smile.

Alice, on the other hand, was totally impressed by the "snazzy Stutz Bearcat." And the more she looked at the car the more she liked Leonard. Almost anyone with that car would have looked as good to her as Rudolph Valentino.

After the standard how do you do's, Alice had a suggestion. "Let's take a drive."

"What about Grace?" asked Leonard.

"Oh, we'll find someone for her," laughed Alice, winking at her sister.

The three roared off in the Stutz, and down the road a bit Grace yelled, "Stop the car, stop the car!" She had spotted a good-looking young blond man trying to hitch a ride. He turned out to be an agreeable companion, and the four proceeded to Proctor's Restaurant in Mount Vernon, where they spent a few hours and twelve dollars of Rhinelander money (equivalent to about $60 in 1976), and later took the girls home. The date was September 20, 1921.

Two days later Leonard received an "It was so nice meeting you" postcard from Alice. Soon afterward he called on her at her home and met her parents. Her mother was white, and when Leonard remarked to Alice, when they were alone, about her father's dark complexion, she answered, "Oh, Daddy's a Cuban Spaniard."

Leonard would later state that he had accepted this explanation without question, and the divorce trial would show that he truly believed it at the time. He was so infatuated with Alice that he was unwilling to believe anything that might stifle the budding romance.

Thereafter he saw Alice once or twice a week and wrote to her on the other days—sometimes three times in a single day. In the course of three years Leonard wrote 763 letters. Alice answered 648 of them. Some of his missives ran to twelve pages. Alice's varied from postcards to five-page letters, many filled with poetry or words from popular songs to express her feelings. Both kept all of each other's letters, and many were read at the trial.

In October 1923, when Leonard began seeing Alice practically every evening, she suggested, "Why not sleep over at the house?" Since he usually stayed until one or two in the morning anyway, it seemed an excellent idea. It also met with the full approval of Alice's parents and her sister Grace, who by now was married to a chauffeur, "Footsy" Miller, and lived in a one-family home adjoining the Joneses'.

The Jones house was a medium-sized wooden-frame dwelling with small bedrooms. Jones and his wife occupied one bedroom and Alice another. There was a very small room off Alice's that provided barely enough space for a bed. Not about to place their distinguished guest in this cubbyhole, the elder Joneses magnanimously gave up their own room, moving their belongings into the closet-sized bedroom.

For Leonard, love was now in full bloom. He was practically a member of the family, and at times he even helped wash and dry dishes. One night he broke three plates. A week later he broke two more. Although he protested vehemently, "It wasn't my fault; they slipped!" this ended his career as an associate dishwasher.

The two lovebirds liked the movies and went to the local cinema quite regularly. However, on December 20, 1923, they decided to vary the fare and attend the theater in New York to see the play everyone was talking about, *Abie's Irish Rose.* Leonard called New York for his father's limousine and chauffeur, instructing the driver to pick him up in Connecticut at the Orchard School. They then drove to Alice's home in New Rochelle.

Leonard intended to return with Alice to the Jones home that same night, but they changed plans on the way to the city. Before going to the theater they checked into the Marie Antoinette Hotel in Manhattan, registering as Mr. and Mrs. James Smith, of Rye, New York.

After a passionate pre-theater encounter, they dressed and went to the play. They could hardly wait for the show to end so they could race back to the hotel. Leonard later claimed that that night was the first time he had experienced the joys of sex, but for Alice the experience was less mindblowing. She may have been less than candid to Leonard about her lineage, but she was unusually truthful regarding other matters. She had written Leonard previously, in one of her many letters, that she had lost her virginity to one Al Rose and regretted that she hadn't "saved it" for Leonard.

They remained at the Marie Antoinette for five glorious

days, except for a grudging three-hour visit Leonard made to his father's midtown home, at 18 West 48th Street, for Christmas dinner. He looked at the dinner as a sort of intermission in what was going on at the hotel, and he was anxious to get back to his "flapper princess."

A month later the lovers again checked into the Marie Antoinette. This time they lingered for two weeks, not leaving the hotel at all, which spoke very well for the charms of Alice and the virility of Leonard. They apparently would have remained longer if Philip Rhinelander, finally aware that Leonard was not at school, but attending to matters other than curing his stuttering, sent private investigators looking for his son.

After an extensive three-day search, they located Leonard. James Moran, one of the investigators, later said, "When we reported to Mr. Rhinelander that his son was staying with a Negress at a hotel he looked ready to pass out. All he could say was, 'This is unbelievable! Impossible! Impossible!' I could almost see his Dutch ancestors holding their heads in their hands and moaning."

To Philip Rhinelander the prospect of a black woman in the hallowed Rhinelander family was absolutely inconceivable. He could literally hear the laughter of his enemies, of whom there were more than a few. Worse would be the "sympathy" sure to flow from his friends. He was determined, at all costs, to break up this romance.

Rhinelander dispatched his friend and lawyer Spotswood D. Bowers to the Marie Antoinette Hotel. "Get that son-of-a-bitch son of mine out of there!"

Bowers subsequently hammered Leonard with threats, intimidation, and arm twisting. Finally the errant blue blood was "persuaded" to leave.

An angry Rhinelander, Sr., then conferred with his long-time friend and advisor James W. Girard (former ambassador to Germany before the United States entered World War I). The strategy they decided on was to ship Leonard off on a six-month cruise from New York to the Bahamas and then through the Panama Canal to Hawaii and the Orient. Philip hoped that by the time his son returned he would have met other young women, developed other interests, and, most important, forgotten Alice.

But Philip Rhinelander could have saved his time and money. Absence only made the heart grow fonder. One week after his return, Leonard and Alice made their move. They were married in the New Rochelle City Hall on October 14, 1924.

The marriage was kept a secret for three weeks. A tip from a City Hall employee to a newspaper friend, John Carter, let the cat out of the bag.

"Are you sure?" asked an astonished Carter.

"Just pay 'em a visit. You'll see for yourself."

Not knowing where Leonard was, the reporter went to the imposing Philip Rhinelander home in New York for details of the wedding. At first Carter was almost turned away at the door. After informing the butler that he had to speak to Mr. Rhinelander "about a very important personal matter," Carter was ushered into the library.

In a few moments Philip Rhinelander appeared and brusquely inquired, "What is this personal matter?"

When Carter asked Rhinelander whether he would supply any of the details of his son's wedding, the old man's face turned ashen; this was the first he had heard anything about it. He didn't say a word. He just stood there, rigid, fists clenched, gritting his teeth. Finally, with a break in his voice, he told Carter, "Please leave. I have nothing to say."

The next day the story exploded in headlines throughout

the country—SOCIALITE MARRIES NEGRESS! It was an incredible bonanza for the tabloid press. As the tale unfolded, the prejudices of whites and the hatred and frustrations of blacks bubbled to the surface like lava from a seething volcano.

When the storm broke Leonard and Alice were living at the Pintard Apartments, at 605 Main Street, New Rochelle. This was a large apartment house, and they had taken four rooms. For three weeks they had lived quietly and happily. Then Leonard, passing a newsstand, spotted the headlines. He knew it was a matter of only a day or two before the Pintard Apartments would be besieged by reporters. The young Rhinelanders surreptitiously left the following morning for the Jones home, where they intended to stay until things blew over.

Philip Rhinelander was now fiercely determined to have the marriage annulled. It had reached the point of obsession. He couldn't believe that Leonard had entered into the union with full knowledge of Alice's color. He felt positive that his son had been deceived and misled with some cock-and-bull story accounting for the "dark appearance" of Alice and other members of her family. Philip believed his son had thereafter engaged in soothing self-deceit and taken refuge in illusion.

The first step was for Rhinelander to retain a law firm to investigate the background of the Jones family to secure proof that they were indeed "colored." He felt that if he could present Leonard with conclusive proof, his son would, as he put it, "come to his senses."

The law firm did not take long to secure the evidence.

Rhinelander then sent his investigators to contact Leonard. They had little trouble locating him, but he refused to speak to them, pleading, "Go away. Go away and leave us alone."

But they stayed put, patiently waiting for him to emerge from the Jones home. After three hours he finally came out and agreed to go for a walk. After a long talk, he was persuaded to agree to see his father later in the week.

On the afternoon of November 11, 1924, a limousine stopped in front of the Jones home to pick up Leonard. He told Alice, "I'll be back tomorrow."

He never returned.

Despite Philip Rhinlander's overbearing and domineering attitude, Leonard had great affection and respect for his father. Philip, greatly hurt by Leonard's apparent disregard for the feelings of his family, still had strong paternal feelings for his son and was determined to prevent him from "wrecking his life."

Leonard was aghast when his father and Leon R. Jacobs, another of his attorneys, hit him with the proof they had assembled that "Alice has Negro blood." Young Rhinelander had believed Alice when she told him her father was a Cuban Spaniard. Of course, he had desperately wanted to believe her. Thereafter he had grown accustomed to the family and their faces and had actually never given it further thought.

Leonard, afraid at first even to look at the data his father's law firm had collected, finally agreed to read it. It revealed that Alice's father, George Jones, when he applied for naturalization, being then a British subject, described himself as a "colored man." In a marriage license issued in 1918 in Pelham, New York, Emily Jones, sister of Alice, was listed as "colored."

At the Travers Island clubhouse of the New York Athletic Club, Mrs. Jane Durham, in charge of the linen, stated that in 1918, Alice had worked in the laundry room for twenty-five dollars a month, including meals. When the United States customs inspectors came to the clubhouse to list aliens because of World War I, they classified Alice as a "mulatto." In a life-insurance application, made for Alice by her mother, Alice was listed as "black."

When full realization came to Leonard, his feelings were not hate, pity, or scorn, but utter confusion and bewilderment. He could have said, "I don't care. I love her. It makes no difference." He didn't; apparently it did make a difference. It was shattering for him, and his world of the last three years was crumbling. He was torn between his former feelings of love for Alice and an awful new feeling akin to repugnance.

He was being brainwashed, and he was confused. His father's auto-suggestive tirades were apparently beginning to work. Leonard later said he felt, as if in a nightmare, that he was running in different directions at the same time. His thinking was adrift in a sea of confusion. He didn't know what to think.

In this completely befuddled and bewildered state of mind, he agreed to start legal proceedings to annul the marriage.

Where the legal remedy of annulment is sought and granted, the marriage is not only ended, it is held never to have come into existence legally. It is the relief granted when the marriage is held to have been induced by fraud. This remedy originated in the ecclesiastical courts, which granted a judgment *vinculum matrimonii* (from the bond of matrimony) and was later adopted by the secular courts.

To Philip Rhinelander it was important that the remedy sought be annulment. It *had* to be! Then, even if Alice were pregnant, her child would never bear the illustrious name of Rhinelander or inherit any of the Rhinelander millions.

The annulment proceedings had become a cause célèbre. It was discussed, sometimes calmly, often heatedly, in restaurants, clubs, taverns, public places, and homes. The tenor was the same. Among whites it was simple, blunt, and cruel—"Can you imagine *him* marrying a nigger?"

The controversy spilled over into politics. Royal S. Copeland, senator from New York, had been asked to state his views on the Rhinelander marriage. At a political meeting, in response to a question, he replied, "In my opinion there is absolutely nothing wrong in the marriage of a Caucasian and a Negro. Absolutely nothing!"

Theodore G. Bilbo, former governor of Mississippi and a future senator from that state, was a prime missionary of racial hatred in the country. He wanted all blacks deported to Liberia, and called on "every red-blooded white man to use any means to keep the nigger away from the polls." He was a fountain perpetually spouting hate and venom. Having been swept into office on the issue of white supremacy, he never let an opportunity go by to make a blatant appeal to the many hatemongers in his constituency.

Meeting Senator Copeland in the Senate restaurant the day after Copeland's statement appeared in the newspapers, Bilbo seized the occasion to play up to his admirers. Shaking a finger in Copeland's face, he said in a blustering falsetto, "Senator, what the hell are you trying to do? Rearrange the world? Everyone knows you're on your knees to the Nigra vote to get elected in New York. That explains the bullshit you handed out yesterday. But I wonder what kind of song you'd be singing if your son married a Nigra!"

Feelings were flaming all over the South, and fiery crosses were being burned by the Ku Klux Klan. Politicians in the North and West soon avoided being quoted on the case. It was a political hot potato, and their evasions were masterpieces of double-talk.

When President Calvin Coolidge was asked at a White House news conference whether he had an opinion about the matter, he said, "I never heard of it," and added, "I have no interest in it whatsoever." That was par for the Coolidge course. At times people in conference with him wondered if he was awake. (On January 5, 1933, Hiram Johnson, senator from California, was informed that Coolidge was dead. "How can they tell?" Johnson asked.)

The first day of the Rhinelander trial hummed with what was described as an almost surrealistic carnival atmosphere. Large crowds gathered early for the available seats, and the circa-1925 Archie Bunkers were quick to point out to each other the "jigs" and "shines" who had the temerity to stand in line with them. "Why don't they stay where they belong?"

When the doors to the courtroom opened the people surged inside as though propelled by a huge gust of wind. There was a mad scramble for seats, and when they were filled the attendants permitted people to stand five and six deep in back of the room. Persons against the wall squirmed like eels, struggling to get a better view of those at the counsel table. There was pushing and jostling and whispers of "There she is," and "There he is," as people excitedly pointed out Alice and Leonard. As the noise level rose the Court Clerk, in a stern voice said, "Quiet in the courtroom!" It took another "Quiet, please!" on a rising note before the noise lessened, but it still did not completely subside.

When Justice Morschauser ascended the bench at ten o'clock he quickly brought decorum, and in nine words ended the discomfort of the standing spectators. "Clear the courtroom, except for those who have seats."

At the counsel table there was an impressive array of talent. Trial counsel for Leonard was ex-Judge Isaac N. Mills, a former Presiding Justice of the Appellate Division. He was wearing a black skullcap and carried a small ear trumpet. A reporter asked a friend of Judge Mills whether these were an affectation being worn for the first time.

"No," was the reply. "The Judge has worn them as long as anyone can remember." Judge Mills's philosophy was that "one must look unusual to be really noticed. Would anyone notice the Leaning Tower of Pisa if it was standing straight?"

The former judge was colorful, extremely competent, and highly respected by the bench and bar. He enjoyed a well-earned reputation for his knowledge of the law and his ability to try a case.

With him at the counsel table was Leon R. Jacobs, the attorney of record for Leonard. Quite a Beau Brummel, all during the three weeks of the trial Jacobs wore a morning coat, striped pants, and spats. He was the family lawyer who handled personal legal matters for Philip Rhinelander.

Against these formidable opponents who would be handling Alice's case? The local chapter of the National Association for the Advancement of Colored People (NAACP) had suggested to Alice that because of the racial overtones of the case and because he was legal counsel for the NAACP, she try to retain Felix Frankfurter, then a professor at the Harvard Law School.

Professor Frankfurter regretfully refused. His law school schedules had previously been seriously disrupted by his extracurricular activities in the Sacco-Vanzetti case in Massachusetts, which led to a period of reserve and coolness between Frankfurter and A. Lawrence Lowell, president of Harvard. Professor Frankfurter apparently preferred not to rekindle old fires.

Alice therefore retained Samuel F. Swinburne, a former judge of the City Court of New Rochelle, to handle the pleadings and motions prior to the trial. As trial counsel Alice retained Lee Parsons Davis, a former District Attorney of Westchester County.

Davis was renowned for his courtroom manner and ability. Among lawyers he was considered creative, brilliant, and innovative. His voice was deep and impressive, and in the courtroom he used it with great dramatic effect.

Physically he was the story-book picture of a lawyer. He moved with grace and ease and resembled Johnny Weismuller, then reigning Olympic champion and sensation of the swimming world.

Judge Mills and his associates had mapped out the Rhinelander strategy. Their whole case rested on their ability to convince a jury that Leonard had been misled into believing that Alice was white. They had to prove the validity of the third paragraph of the plaintiff's complaint, which read,

> 3. That the consent of said plaintiff to such marriage was obtained by fraud. That prior to such marriage the defendant represented to and told the plaintiff that she was white and not colored and had no colored blood, which representations the plaintiff believed to be true and was induced thereby to consent to said marriage and entered into such marriage relying on such representations, which representations plaintiff discovered to be wholly untrue.

Although hatemongers felt that Rhinelander had a strong case—to them it seemed little more than, in vulgar street jargon, a matter of "the bitch misled the poor bastard into thinking she was white, didn't she?"—shrewd Judge Mills knew better. He realized only too well that Rhinelander's case was weak. The jury would be seeing Alice every day, and they would also observe her father and sisters. The whole family, except the mother, was obviously "colored." Mills was quite certain the jury's reaction would be: "Was the plaintiff blind or an imbecile not to have seen it? How *could* he have been misled?"

Judge Mills knew that most jurors made an honest effort to decide a case solely on the evidence and would be guided by a judge's charge to disregard anything not presented by witnesses as evidence. But he also knew that in some cases jurors could not divorce themselves from the unconscious workings of their minds. Minds are not like magnetic tape from which information may be erased at will.

For a judge to order remarks or testimony "stricken from the record," and to order jurors to erase from their minds what they have seen or heard, in certain instances is as effective in result as King Canute ordering the tide to roll back. And just as the tide kept rolling on in spite of Canute's command, so would some juror's minds keep rolling on in spite of anything a judge could say.

Appellate Courts have held that there are matters a Court cannot later erase from jurors' minds by instructions. "You cannot unring the bell that's been rung."

Mills felt sure that in this case, after the jurors had seen and heard the Jones family, their one thought would remain —"How could Leonard *not* have known?"

Mills knew he had no easy mountain to climb. But he had climbed hard mountains before, and quite often he had reached peaks that had been thought unscalable.

At 10:45 A.M. on November 12, 1925, Judge Mills took the first step in climbing the newest mountain. He began his opening statement to the jury.

The opening statement of counsel to a jury is of great importance. It enables a lawyer to present to them the nature of the case, the issues involved, and the facts he intends to prove. It is equivalent to the synopsis of a story. It makes it easier for the jury to understand the testimony as it is brought out.

Judge Mills began his opening statement with a confident air and in a low conversational voice. He told the jury he would prove that "Rhinelander was pursued by Alice and duped into marriage." He said he would show that this was an unsophisticated young man whose schooling, because of his speech defect, was not the best and that it would even be possible to characterize him as a little "brain-tied." Further, Mills said, Leonard was very naïve and believed almost anything anyone told him. Alice, from the very first, had made up her mind that she would snare Leonard into marriage by using the wiles of sex, and she had completely enslaved him to her sexually by enticing him to stay at the Marie Antoinette Hotel.

Despite the sexual enslavement, Mills went on, Leonard "never would have married her had she told him she was colored, and this deception was furthered by her entire family. We will show the kind of people they are. Mixed marriages are a terrible thing when entered into knowingly. They are *monstrous* when entered into by deception. White is white, and black is black. We can't change it, and we *shouldn't* change it."

The air was charged and Mills forged ahead. He said Alice had lied when she told Leonard she was white. Had she told the truth, "there never would have been a marriage, and we would not be in this courtroom today. All the representations about her color were false, and the consent to the marriage was obtained by fraud. We will prove all of that to you."

Mills slowly walked back to the counsel table.

Lee Parsons Davis rose and walked to the jury box. In a booming voice, he blasted away. "When Judge Mills spoke, a wave of anger swept over me. It will not be my purpose to unnecessarily hurt Rhinelander or his father. I shall attempt to try this case cleanly. But Judge Mills in his adroitness is trying an entirely different case. In my twenty years at the bar I have never listened to a more *vicious* opening, a more *cruel* opening, or a more *un-American opening.*"

Davis declared that he would fight "without kid gloves," and if Mills wished to throw mud he would throw a little also. In reply to Mills's attack on the Jones family he said, "If Leonard did not know the color of the family he was marrying into he did not suffer from being 'brain-tied' as much as he did from blindness." Rhinelander had not only put the elder Jones out of his bed, continued Davis, but "he ate the Jones meals, dandled a Jones grandchild on his knees, and generally became a member of the household." *How could he not have known?* That became Davis's theme, and he hammered at it.

Judge Mills, said Davis, was trying to prove his client was merely a naïve babe in the woods. "Maybe he was, but the issue in this case isn't whether Rhinelander was naïve or sophisticated. We are here to determine whether Alice misled him into believing that she was white. All we have to determine," noted Davis sarcastically, "is not whether Rhinelander was brilliant or dumb, or whether he was 'brain-tied' so that he stuttered and stammered, but only whether he was *blind!* If Judge Mills can show us that Rhinelander was blind then I would say it is possible that the plaintiff could have been misled. But if Rhinelander was not blind, how could he have been misled? If he could see, how could he have been misled? How could Alice have misled Rhinelander into thinking black was white! And that, gentlemen of the jury, is what this case is all about."

Judge Mills's plan was to portray Leonard as weak minded —one who was easily led, misled, and deceived. He would attempt to show that his client had been pursued and duped into marriage by a conniving, strong-willed Alice Jones, who had seen and seized an opportunity to marry into one of America's wealthiest families. This portrayal of Leonard as a village idiot would humiliate both Leonard and the Rhinelander family, but that did not cause Mills to lose any sleep. It was the only approach to take, under the circumstances. As Mills pointed out to Rhinelander, Sr., "The only way to make an omelet is to break eggs."

The first witness for the plaintiff was Dr. L. Pierce Clark, of 2 East 65th Street, Manhattan. Dr. Clark conducted the Orchard, the school to which Leonard went for his stuttering. He was a specialist in nervous and mental disorders.

During the first day's medical testimony Leonard sat at the counsel table, staring ahead glumly. His pinched, tanned face wore absolutely no expression. If he cared what was going on around him in the occasional sprightly exchanges between counsel, which drew laughter from the audience, he gave no sign of it. Alice, on the other hand, watched the proceedings with interest, at times with a smile. On occasion she bent her head to her handkerchief and dabbed at her eyes.

When Dr. Clark completed his testimony, spectators stared curiously at Leonard. Could he even be trusted to cross a street by himself? The picture Clark had painted was clearly of a person none too bright. Backward, in fact.

However, on cross-examination by Davis, Doctor Clark was forced to admit that although he portrayed Leonard as shy and extremely bashful in the presence of women, which was the basis of his conclusion that Leonard was "backward," there were times when Leonard was the "life of the party."

"Using your previous yardstick for declaring that in your

opinion Leonard Rhinelander was 'backward,' would his being the 'life of the party' make him a genius?" asked Davis.

"Not a genius," answered Clark. "Only less backward."

"Why not put it the other way," said Davis; "why not say he is a genius who is a little backward? A backward genius."

"I can't go along with that," Clark said seriously, as spectators laughed.

The moment everyone was waiting for came when Judge Mills called Leonard Rhinelander to the witness stand.

"Do you swear to tell the truth, the whole truth, and nothing but the truth, so help you God?" intoned the court clerk.

"I d-d-do," answered Leonard, hand on the Bible.

Leonard was not a prepossessing figure on the stand, peering through heavy glasses with an expression of bewilderment in his eyes. To put him at ease, Judge Mills asked him to state his name and address for the record.

Then he asked Leonard questions that led him through a recital of his meeting with Alice, her invitation to him to call on her, his subsequent visits several times a week, her letters, the theater trip that had resulted in his spending five days with her at the Marie Antoinette Hotel, and a second stay there of two weeks. Leonard recounted all the details of the affair in the same expressionless, stuttering manner.

Philip Rhinelander never attended a single session of the trial but had little difficulty following its progress. It was on front pages of all newspapers in New York and in most throughout the country.

Embarrassing as the debacle may have been for the Rhinelanders, Philip's peers were in no position to throw stones. Many of the blue-blood clans had skeletons buried deep in their closets. Posh private sanitariums were filled with alcoholic or mentally unbalanced millionaries and sons and daughters of millionaires, whose problems were every bit as "embarrassing" to their families as the Rhinelander scandal. The only difference, for the most part, was that the others had managed to stay out of the newspapers.

Meeting several friends, including Walter Teagle, president of the Standard Oil Company of New Jersey (Exxon today) at the Bankers Club at 120 Broadway in Manhattan, Philip Rhinelander was not offended when the topic delicately came around to the Rhinelander trial. Artists' renditions of Leonard on the witness stand were in the papers, and Leonard, in his testimony, had hardly covered the Rhinelanders with glory. Having had a few drinks the group was in a somewhat uninhibited mood and Teagle said to Rhinelander, "Philip, when Leonard was born, are you sure you got the right baby at the hospital?"

After Leonard's first day on the stand Judge Mills entered into three days of continuous reading of Alice's letters. At times they were highly interesting; at times, highly boring. Even the jury, desirous of doing their duty and listening, eventually began nodding and yawning as Judge Mills read and read and read.

They were the unrestrained letters of an illiterate girl, deeply moved by conflicting emotions and desires. They contained poems and words of popular songs to express her feelings. They contained hopes for automobiles and money and an apartment of her own. They rang with cries of hope and fear and envy. Her thoughts of love and money were so joined together that in one revealing letter she wrote, "I dreamed of you last night . . . and how you loved me, and you gave me piles and piles of ten-dollar bills. But you could not give me enough of them, and every one of them was brand-new."

In all, Mills read more than a hundred letters into the record, but the judge, jury, and spectators were saved from hearing dozens more thanks to the action of "a person or persons unknown." Judge Mills left a batch of thirty letters on the counsel table when the court called a fifteen-minute recess at 11:15 A.M. Returning at 11:30, an astonished Mills found the letters gone.

A smiling Lee Parsons Davis disavowed any knowledge of them and gently suggested that someone who couldn't stand the thought of listening to another letter had gone temporarily insane and was probably eating them somewhere. "And," added Davis, "as I haven't found the letters read thus far very appetizing, I fear the purloined ones are no better and might have upset everyone's stomachs."

The letters were never found, but Judge Mills had little trouble producing another bundle from a seemingly unlimited store.

The last letters were read into the record the third day: letters pleading, cajoling, threatening, suggesting; letters that aroused pity, anger, and disgust.

Judge Mills recalled Leonard to the stand, to go into a recital of the falsehoods that Alice had given him to account for the dark skin of her father and herself. He then asked Leonard his final series of questions, "Did Alice Jones tell you that her father was a Cuban Spaniard?"

"Yes, she did."

"Did you ever speak to Mr. Jones about his color?"

"Yes, I did."

"What did he say?"

"He said he was an Englishman with the jaundice."

After the laughter had subsided, Judge Mills continued, "Did Alice tell you that she was white?"

"Yes, she did."

"Would you have married her had you known she was colored?"

"No, I would not."

"Have you since the marriage learned that she is colored?"

"Yes, I have."

"Have you lived with her since you learned she was colored?"

"No. I have not."

"That is all," said Judge Mills.

Leonard was now to face Lee Parsons Davis for cross-examination. Leonard had been apprehensive about this moment. He had been told that Davis was devastating and that the only way to cope with him was to relax, take time in answering, and never volunteer anything beyond the answer to the question. This was good advice, but it was extremely difficult for Leonard to follow so far as relaxing was concerned.

As he watched Davis approach, Rhinelander resembled a frightened bird looking at a cobra—he was almost paralyzed with fear.

Davis gazed at Leonard. It was obvious Davis welcomed the opportunity that had been so long in arriving. Luckily for Rhinelander's taut nerves, the lawyer began on a soft note that enabled Leonard to unfreeze a bit.

"Because of the impediment in your speech I want to be as kindly as I can," Davis said slowly. "If you do not understand what I say tell me and I will repeat it gladly. Now, tell me, your mind is all right now, isn't it?"

"I think it is," said Leonard warily.

"You don't want Judge Mills and the jury to get the impression that you are an imbecile?"

Rhinelander folded back his arms and with an effort, as if to regain control of his nerves, said, "No."

"Back in 1923 your mind was all right, wasn't it?"

"Yes."

"You knew what you were doing?"

"Yes."

"Back in 1922 and 1921 your mind was all right?"

"Yes."

"You don't want this jury to get the idea you didn't know what you were doing?"

"No."

With these six questions and Rhinelander's responses, Davis laid the foundation to decimate the image Judge Mills had so painstakingly attempted to build—that his client did not know what he was doing.

Davis now proceeded to use that groundwork to batter and bludgeon Leonard in three days of cross-examination, with the simple theme of "How could you not have known that Alice was 'colored'?" He enmeshed Rhinelander in a mass of contradictions regarding his acts and relations with Alice that would have been plausible only if Leonard did not know what he was doing.

Davis kept on hammering, "You said you knew what you were doing. Did you or didn't you?"

"Yes, I did," was the repeated, anguished answer.

Judge Mills looked on impassively, but inside he was seething.

After two days on the stand Leonard's face wore a continuous expression of bewilderment. He hardly resembled the popular image of a bon-vivant blue blood. When he attempted to speak, it was with a violent physical effort, which showed in his tensed muscles. His hands clasped and unclasped over his knees, and when he answered his words shot forth spasmodically, brokenly, sometimes in a rapid mumble that would compel the court stenographer to request that the answer be repeated.

The gleaming intensity in Rhinelander's eyes indicated the

great effort he made at concentration to overcome his speech impediment. Occasionally his eyelids opened and closed rapidly, and his mouth strained until his lips were a thin straight line before he was able to speak.

At the end of the day Leonard was exhausted, physically and mentally. He welcomed the four-o'clock adjournment almost with tears.

An interested spectator at the trial was Bernard Baruch, the internationally known financier. He was a long-time friend of Judge Mills, and since everyone was talking about the Rhinelander case Baruch had decided to attend the session during the cross-examination of Leonard.

At the end of the session, walking to a restaurant for an early dinner before driving back to New York, Baruch was cornered by reporters.

"What do you think about the way the case is going?" Baruch was asked.

"What do *you* think?" Baruch replied.

"I think it's curtains for Rhinelander," said one reporter. "This lawyer Davis is teriffic. You don't have to be a genius to get his drift. How could Rhinelander not have known the Joneses were colored? He saw them every day, and he saw Alice naked."

Baruch smiled. "Davis could be wrong," he said. "Just because you see a thing every day doesn't mean you really see what you are looking at. Sometimes you don't."

"That sounds like a riddle, Mr. Baruch. A sort of shell game—now you see it, now you don't."

"No," said Baruch. "That isn't what I mean. Let me give you an illustration. How many times in the last three years have you handled a five- or ten-dollar bill? I could say in the last thirty years, but let's make it the last three years, the same length of time Leonard has known Alice. How many times have some of you seen and handled these bills?"

"Hundreds of times," said one of the reporters. "But what are you getting at, Mr. Baruch? What has that to do with this case?"

Baruch smiled again. "All right. Let's say you've seen at least one of the bills every day. That means you have seen them at least one thousand times in the last three years. Right? Well, whose picture is on a five-dollar bill, and whose is on a ten?"

"I don't know!" was the reply, almost in unison.

"But you've looked at them every day," said Baruch. "Didn't you see the faces? How could you not know?"

Baruch had made his point. In a surprised tone, a reporter remarked, "You sound just like Davis."

"Furthermore," continued Baruch, relishing the impact of his observations, "you've seen thousands of five- and ten-dollar bills, and yet you really didn't see them, although you looked at them. And you've seen the reverse side of the bills almost as often, but if your life depended on it I'll bet you couldn't tell me what's on *that* side of it. And that's just what Rhinelander was doing. He was looking at the Jones family every day and was looking at Alice, but he really wasn't noticing anything, any more than you did when you looked at the bills."

"They should have made you Secretary of the Treasury instead of chairman of the War Industries Board," joked one reporter.

"Does anybody really notice what they are looking at?" asked another newsman.

"Do you mean with five- and ten-dollar bills? Only about five people out of a hundred, I'd say. There was once a study made on it by a Midwestern university, but I don't remember the exact figure. It may be less than 5 percent. And the point is that when it comes to looking at people, I doubt if he percentage is much higher. Picasso, the great painter, has said more than once, 'Why assume that to look is to see?'

"So you see," Baruch went on, "Davis could be wrong, harping on the fact that since Leonard saw them every day he must have known. That's not necessarily the way the mind works. In fact, after a time the more Leonard saw the Jones family the *less* he might notice. After all, do parents who see their children every day notice the changes in them as they are growing up? Suddenly they're grown up! Do married people notice any change in each other as the changes are taking place? They change considerably, but do they notice the change? If Davis were to put these married people on the stand and say, 'You've seen each other every day. How could you not have noticed the changes that took place?' Couldn't they truthfully answer, 'We didn't, we just didn't.' But according to Davis they would be lying."

The reporters laughed, and one remarked, "Maybe *you* ought to be in there trying the case!"

Davis resumed his examination of Leonard immediately after the morning session opened.

"Mr. Rhinelander, I would like to go back to the time you first met Alice. You say that Alice pursued you and made all the advances?"

"Yes."

"And you did not make any?"

"No."

"I will read to you from a letter that you wrote Alice, dated October 7, 1921. I quote: 'If you are real nice to me once in a while I will let you drive.' What did you mean by that?"

"If she would let me caress her I would let her drive the car."

"So on October 7, two weeks after you first met this girl, with all your proclaimed sex innocence, you were trying to get her mind on sex, weren't you?"

"Yes," Rhinelander admitted. He seemed a little dazed, and he stared at Judge Mills, who quietly looked away.

Davis continued to hammer. "I will read to you from a letter you sent to Alice a month later. I quote: 'Now, baby, remember what I asked you to do for me about getting a little apartment in New York. Do try your best to do it, because I want you. Suppose we take a trip to New York on Friday and see what we can find.' Were you very innocent when you suggested getting the apartment?"

"Yes," answered Leonard, as spectators tittered.

"You weren't really innocent when you met Alice, were you?"

"Yes, I was."

"You made love to Alice? You weren't so innocent as not to know how to make love, were you?"

"Yes, I was."

Davis, half-smiling, looked over at the jury. They were listening intently.

"Well, let's see, Mr. Rhinelander. You knew how to hold her hand, didn't you?"

"Yes."

"You knew how to put your arm around her?"

"Yes."

"You knew how to kiss her?"

"Yes."

"How did you make love?"

"We rode around in my automobile."

"You made love in your automobile?"

"Yes."

"It amused you to put your arm around her and kiss her?"

"Yes."

"You got a thrill from it?"

"Yes."

"You didn't know when you first put your arm around her and kissed her that you would get a thrill from it?"

"No."

"Well, how did you know enough to put your arm around her and kiss her?"

"Human instinct, I guess."

"You had a sex urge, didn't you, while making love to Alice?"

"Yes," said Leonard. His hand shaking, he drank some water, spilling a little.

"What did you do to play on that sex urge in Alice?"

Leonard remained silent. The pause was so long that Davis suggested that Rhinelander be permitted to take a rest, but Justice Morschauser directed that the examination go on.

All this time Judge Mills sat quietly in front of his client, raising no objection. Alice sat at the end of the counsel table in front of the jury box. She had removed her hat and patted her hair into place, and she stared defiantly at Leonard.

Davis continued his questioning. "You understand, Mr. Rhinelander, there is no more room for modesty in this case after what you put this girl through in reading her letters in this courtroom. How long after you met Alice was it that you became intimate with her?"

Rhinelander was biting his lower lip and hunching and twisting his shoulders, as if to straighten out a muscle. He squirmed and drank a huge gulp of water. He tried to speak, but uttered an unintelligible mumble.

"Mr. Rhinelander, did you understand the question? Do you know what is meant by being intimate with a girl?"

"Yes."

Davis was now relentless. "Mr. Rhinelander, I repeat the

question. How long after you met Alice was it that you became intimate with her? How long was it?"

"About one month," said Leonard, in a voice that could hardly be heard. He was trying to reach for the glass of water, but his hand was shaking so much that he could not hold the glass.

Judge Mills's groundwork of Leonard's innocence and his contention that Alice had pursued Leonard were sinking fast.

Davis proceeded to put Leonard through the wringer with dozens of contradictions between testimony he had given on direct examination and the admissions he was now forced to make. He requested permission of the Court to read two more of the letters Leonard had written Alice. "Judge Mills has read over one hundred letters from the defendant to the plaintiff. I would like to read just two more that *he* wrote to *her*," said Davis.

After a conversation with counsel at the bench, Justice Morschauser said, "I want to give every woman a chance to leave this courtroom. If I were a woman I would not want to stay in the room and hear these letters." He then instructed the court attendant to put out all young persons present.

When Davis was about ready to read the first of the two letters, Justice Morschauser had a further thought and requested counsel to approach the bench again. He asked Davis for a copy of the letter he was about to read. After looking at it the judge's eyebrows arched. He cleared his throat and said, "I can no longer leave it to the discretion of the women whether or not to stay. I must order that all ladies leave this room."

The judge's concern for the delicate ears of the fair sex excited some laughter and whispered comments among the male spectators that whatever was in the letters, many of the women had heard it before. A pounding gavel quickly brought order.

Davis read the first letter. It was highly erotic. He asked Rhinelander, "You recognize that letter as pure, unadulterated smut, don't you?"

"Yes."

Davis then read the second letter. "And when you wrote *this* letter you knew it was the vilest kind of suggestive smut, didn't you?"

"Yes," said Leonard quietly.

"You knew what you were doing, what you were writing?" asked Davis, his voice rising.

"Yes."

"Going back to your stays at the Marie Antoinette Hotel. That was your idea, wasn't it?"

"No," Leonard said defiantly. "It was Alice's."

Davis, shaking a hand in anger, roared at him, "Is there anything vile in this case that you are not putting up to this girl to drag her through the slime?"

"She deceived me," stuttered Rhinelander, angered at Davis's shouting.

"When you saw her in the hotel you saw her unclothed, didn't you?"

Leonard's answer hardly surprised the spectators. "Yes," he said.

"Did you then know she was colored?" Davis asked sarcastically.

"No, I did not," was the reply.

There was laughter in the courtroom, and the judge quickly pounded his gavel.

"At this point, Your Honor," said Davis, "I would like to interrupt the examination of Mr. Rhinelander and, with the plaintiff and counsel present, have the jury see the body of

Alice Jones Rhinelander in the juryroom. I believe it would be proper at this time in view of the plaintiff's answer to my last question. I know the request is somewhat unusual. However, it relates to the testimony of the witness and goes to the heart of the matter of the alleged fraud and misrepresentation the plaintiff alleges."

After strenuous objections by Judge Mills that this was highly improper, Justice Morschauser ruled, "I will allow it."

An understandably nervous and embarrassed Alice Rhinelander was then instructed, "Please go to the juryroom and disrobe to the waist." This manner of "viewing the evidence" would have almost as much written about it as the sinking of the *Lusitania*.

After being viewed by the jury as almost a statue on exhibition, a distraught and crying Alice remained in the juryroom for an hour after everyone left. Her mother came in to cheer her up and remained to weep with her.

Upon the return of the jury to the courtroom, Davis resumed his questioning. "Your wife's body, which the jury has just seen, is the same shade as when you saw her in the Marie Antoinette?"

"Yes."

"And you still say that you did not then know she was colored?"

"Yes."

Davis, standing in front of the jury box, looked slowly at the jury. He then turned to Leonard and repeated, "And you still say that you did not know she was colored?"

"Yes," replied Leonard, almost in a whisper.

Davis again slowly turned to face the jury, allowing Leonard's answer to sink in. Davis's expression seemed to say, "You have just seen the defendant in the juryroom, unclothed to the waist. Now the witness is telling you he thought black was white. Can you now really believe he did not know?"

Davis turned back to Leonard, stared at him, and said almost contemptuously, "That is all."

Leonard's ordeal was over—for the moment. He gulped and swallowed hard. He had never felt worse in his life.

With the completion of Leonard's testimony and cross-examination, Judge Mills rested his case. Davis made the usual motions to dismiss, which Justice Morschauser denied. The case was adjourned to 10 A.M. the following day, when Davis was to start with his defense witnesses. The first was expected to be Alice Rhinelander.

Leaving the courthouse with Davis at the end of the day of merciless cross-examination of Leonard, Judge Mills said, "Lee, you're doing a masterful job, and I have to commend you. A masterful job! But aren't you harping too much on just two aspects? You can't write a song with two notes, you know."

"Are you sure of that?" Davis asked with a smile.

"Well, Lee, frankly, when it comes to you I'm not sure of anything. But if I'm forced to give an answer it would have to be that it can't be done."

Davis couldn't help laughing. "Judge, that wasn't fair. I trapped you into that answer. But it has been done, and in a rather big way. You see, the entire melody of Beethoven's first movement of his Fifth Symphony is based on just two notes. Check it, Judge. It's true. I hope my Rhinelander melody goes over as well as Beethoven's did."

Mills wondered if it was a harbinger of things to come. As he told an associate at a meeting later that evening, "That's some melody that Davis is composing in the courtroom. It's a two-note John Philip Sousa march, and he's marching us right out of the courthouse!"

Judge Mills and his associates met at his office at seven o'clock that night to map the next day's strategy. Mills told them he was very disturbed. Davis's cross-examination of Leonard, he felt, had had a tremendous impact on the jury. Obviously, the allegations of Alice's fraud and deception were almost farcical in the light of what was developing at the trial. As he said, "If I pointed out a horse to a person and said, 'That's a cow,' only an idiot would believe it. We're now in that position."

Judge Mills felt that he had to conjure up a new theory if the case was to have a chance of survival.

The discussion was immersed in gloom. One of his associates, attempting optimism, said, "Judge, you can't lose this case. Stop worrying."

Mills replied, "They also said that the *Titanic* couldn't sink." The laugh that followed broke the tension.

After a few hours they evolved an ingenious new theory.

At 10 A.M. spectators heard the now familiar "All rise." With the appearance of Judge Morschauser, the Court was in session. "Be seated," intoned the court attendant.

Mills rose and advised the Court he had a motion to make. He moved to amend the complaint with an allegation of "negative fraud." In other words, he said, he wished to charge that while Rhinelander may not have believed his wife to be colored, the defendant was guilty of negative fraud when she did not affirmatively tell him that she was "colored."

Mills went on to state that the old procedure in amending a complaint during a trial was to withdraw a juror and go to Special Term for an amendment to the complaint, but this would result in a mistrial. However, he did not want a mistrial. He argued that under the new rules of Civil Procedure it was possible for Justice Morschauser to permit an amendment, so that it would be permissable for Mills to argue that

Alice should have told her husband she was colored before he married her.

This motion presented a dilemma for both sides. If Mills was to have a mistrial declared, it would indicate a weak case and a completely changed theory. His inclusion that Alice *should* have told Leonard would raise problems in the pleadings and his proof. But he felt the present jury might be confused enough to resolve their findings of fact in his client's favor, whereas a new jury might not be confused at all.

Davis, on the other hand, did not want a mistrial because he felt this jury was favorable and would resolve the findings of fact for Alice, so that Justice Morschauser would render a decision in her favor. He did not want to open the way for a new complaint, with a new trial and another jury—he felt a new complaint would definitely be more difficult to oppose.

He objected strenuously to permitting the amendment at this juncture, inasmuch as his whole theory of the case had been based upon a complaint alleging affirmative fraud. But the last thing he wanted was a mistrial and a new jury. He therefore told Justice Morschauser, "Although I do not feel Your Honor can permit the amendment, I will waive technicalities."

Davis made it very clear that this was being done to avoid a mistrial and added, "First they say she said too much, and now they say she said nothing. Judge Mills wants two strings to his bow. I won't quarrel over the technicalities involved, but I feel that in asking an amendment at this late date they are guilty of laxity."

Justice Morschauser said he would take the matter under advisement and render his decision the next morning. He indicated, however, that he would grant a motion by Mills to end the case by withdrawing a juror and having a mistrial declared, if that was what he wanted. The case was then adjourned to the next day.

Judge Mills left the courtroom on the horns of a dilemma. He appeared sunk if the case continued, and if he now launched another boat he had no assurance that it would not wind up with as many leaks as this one. If the Court denied his motion he had to make a fateful decision.

His mind wandered to the Hamlet soliloquy, "To be or not to be." Only, to continue or not, to have a mistrial or not, *those* were the questions.

Mills knew his problems in this case. They couldn't possibly be fewer if he started another action, and they might be greater. He had learned from sad experience that when matters were running negatively, if anything could possibly go wrong it usually did.

On the other hand, a new trial would be a brand-new ballgame. In the current one he was now far behind, and he would need a home run with the bases loaded to stand a chance. He just didn't know who was capable of hitting that home run, and he didn't have anyone on base. The game was in the late innings. Time was running out.

The next morning Justice Morschauser saved Mills the necessity of making a decision and agonizing whether it was right. The Judge ruled that Mills had the right to amend the complaint to include an additional charge that Alice had been guilty of negative fraud in *not* telling Leonard she was colored.

Davis raised only a perfunctory exception to the ruling and requested that in view of the amended complaint he be permitted to recall Rhinelander to the stand before he called witnesses for the defense. Justice Morschauser granted the request.

As Leonard sat down in the witness chair, Davis smiled

broadly at Judge Mills, who muttered to his law clerk, sitting beside him, "What the hell is he up to now?"

Standing near the jury box, Davis then slowly went to the counsel table to pick up a paper. He again glanced over at Mills, and with a shock Mills realized that Davis was struggling to keep from laughing.

Mills now knew that for some reason Davis welcomed the amended complaint. He also knew that Leonard was in for a rough session he would not have been subjected to if the complaint had not been amended. Mills's instinct told him that somehow he had put Leonard's neck in a noose, and Davis was going to pull it tight.

"Here it comes," whispered Mills to an associate. "Davis has latched on to something."

Davis smiled pleasantly at Leonard, increasing Mill's foreboding. "Mr. Rhinelander, do you still contend that your wife told you that she was white?" asked Davis.

"Yes, I do."

"And now you claim she deceived you by saying nothing about being colored?"

"Yes."

"And you heard nothing from anyone about her color?"

"No, I did not."

"You are sure of that?"

"Yes, I am."

"You are positive of that?"

"Yes, I am."

Davis then sprang his trap. "Do you know the whereabouts of the chauffeur who drove you and Alice to the Marie Antoinette Hotel?"

"No, I do not," answered Leonard, looking briefly at Mills. "I haven't any idea."

Davis asked Leonard to identify a clock he had given Alice

as a Christmas present. Leonard had given Alice so many gifts, why ask him about a clock? wondered Mills. What was so important about that?

He was soon to learn.

Davis waved Rhinelander from the stand. "That is all."

Judge Mills then again announced, "The plaintiff rests."

Davis renewed his motion to dismiss, which Justice Morschauser denied. The defendant's case would now begin.

Like many great trial lawyers, Davis was a master showman. Everyone in the courtroom sensed that something dramatic was about to take place, and Davis did not disappoint them. His voice rang out, "Bring the witness in!"

There was a commotion at the doors to the courtroom, and a young man in a brown working jacket walked in, went to the witness stand, and held up his hand to be sworn.

Davis, not smiling now, looked over at Mills. He had an intent expression, and Mills had a feeling that a bomb was about to fall. He fervently wished he had had a mistrial declared when he had the chance. He also wished he had taken a Bromo-Seltzer that morning.

The witness was Ross Chidester, the former Rhinelander chauffuer, who was now working in White Plains for a baking company. In answer to questions Chidester stated that he had been employed by Philip Rhinelander as a chauffuer for a year and a half, that he knew Alice Jones, and that he had driven her about with Leonard. He said he had seen all the Jones family in their home.

"Have you seen Mr. Jones in his house?" asked Davis.

"Yes, I have."

"You saw his color?"

"Yes, I did."

"What was he?"

"He was colored."

"Did you see other members of the family?"

"Yes, I did."

"What color were they?"

"Except for the mother they were colored."

"Do you recall the day you drove Rhinelander and Alice to the Marie Antoinette Hotel?"

"Yes, I do."

"Will you please tell us what happened?" asked Davis.

Chidester recalled the details vividly. He had gone to Stamford to pick up Rhinelander and waited for him in his room while he packed.

"During the course of the packing did he show you anything?" asked Davis.

"Yes, a clock," was the reply. The witness then pointed out the clock Rhinelander had identified a few minutes earlier.

"What did he say?" asked Davis.

"He said, 'Ross, I want to show you a Christmas present for Alice.'"

"What did you say to that?"

"I said, 'Do you mean you bought a Christmas present for her?' He said, 'Yes.'"

"And then what did you say?"

"I said, 'Don't you know her father is a colored man? Don't you know Alice is colored?'"

"And what did he say?" Davis asked slowly.

"He said, 'I know it, and I don't give a damn if they are.'"

There was a collective gasp from the spectators.

Davis then asked Chidester what happened next, and he replied, "I told Leonard I felt like taking him out on the lawn in front of the school and kicking the stuffing out of him. Only I used a different word than *stuffing*."

This brought a titter from the spectators. Judge Mills, how-ever, was not laughing. The worst had happened. The jury now had sworn testimony that Leonard had knowledge of Alice's color. While they could have speculated before that he must have known from the surrounding circumstances, this was the first testimony actually introduced that Leonard in fact did know.

While there was no testimony that Alice herself had ad-mitted it to Leonard, Mills was almost certain that when the jury finally went to the juryroom to deliberate, their rationale would be, "We now have testimony that Rhine-lander knew she was colored. How could he have been misled?" They no longer would have to speculate. As far as this jury was concerned Mills's pleading Leonard's ignorance of Alice's color would have the impact of a feather landing on a pillow.

Judge Mills cross-examined Chidester harshly and at length, but he couldn't shake him in the least. The chauffeur's story stood up "like the Rock of Gibraltar," as Davis said later.

Mills did not dare put Leonard back on the stand to rebut Chidester's testimony. It rang too true. And, reasoned Mills, if Leonard became flustered and admitted the con-versations with Chidester, they might as well pack up and go home. It was almost all over now, but there was still a tiny spark of hope. "Davis might stumble," observed Mills. It was only a chance, but the best of lawyers could blow a case that seemed impossible to lose.

But Mills realistically felt the possibility of Leonard's win-ning this case was about the same as the possibility of the country electing a black President to follow Coolidge.

At this juncture the only conceivable obstacle to Davis's winning the case was a weird verdict. Mills knew from long experience that juries sometimes returned weird verdicts, and now that was his solitary ray of hope. After all his years as a judge and lawyer he now had to pin his hopes of winning the case on such an unlikely verdict. What an outlook!

While on the bench Judge Mills had found himself in accord with 90 percent of the jury verdicts in his Court, and he had great respect for the jury system. But he knew juries sometimes reached unbelievable conclusions on the evidence. Some could be laid to prejudice against a litigant, some to sympathy, and some to the jury venting its spleen for a variety of reasons.

Some jury verdicts are outright miscarriages of justice, and this has happened often enough to be a cause of great concern to the judiciary. It is not unusual, years after a jury has brought in a guilty verdict in a criminal case, for a belated confession by the actual guilty party to clear the convicted unforunate. But years in jail can never be brought back.

Then there were those verdicts which defied explanation. Some were cases of corruption—outright bribery of a juror or jurors. But that was not an indictment of the jury system any more than corruption of judges was an indictment of the judicial system.

Many judges have strayed from the path of virtue. Among them was Justice Albert Cardozo of the New York State Supreme Court, who resigned after numerous charges of bribery and corruption were brought against him in an impeachment proceeding. And yet his son, Benjamin N. Cardozo, became Chief Judge of the New York Court of Appeals, and later an Associate Justice of the Supreme Court of the United States, acclaimed and honored as one of the most renowned legal scholars and respected jurists this country has known.

The Federal judiciary, even at a high level, has not been

Blueblood "Kip" Rhinelander discovered wife Alice "had Negro blood." Their divorce was perhaps the most explosive in American history.

A pensive Alice Rhinelander, and her mother, in court. It was a nightmare for both.

James Stillman, the ultra-dignified president of the biggest bank in the country, and his lovely wife Anne led private lives that shocked the nation when details were revealed in the divorce courts.

Twenty-two-year-old Barbara Hutton and her brazenly opportunistic first husband, Russian-born Prince Alexis Mdivani. ("If you owned three goats you were royalty in *his* part of Russia," scoffed observers.) She paid him $2 million to marry her, and got what she wanted: a title.

Barbara with husband #2, Count Court Haugwitz Reventlow. He was the father of her only child, Lance. The marriage was kaput by 1938. Reventlow was ever afterwards "a disgruntled ex-husband."

With husband #3, Cary Grant. He was the only one of Barbara's seven mates she didn't have to pay for. To everyone's surprise, however, she was telephoning a "secret suitor" right up to their marriage.

World War II forced Barbara into her "Hollywood phase." Here she and Grant flank bride Rosalind Russell and groom Frederick Brisson at their 1941 wedding. Cary had introduced the couple.

With Prince Igor Troubetzkoy, husband #4. Blackmail eventually reared its ugly head. Barbara and the Prince parted the worst of friends.

At 41 Barbara married Porfirio Rubirosa, the most sought after and well-endowed stud in the international stable in the early 1950s. Never before—and never again—would a man cause her to suffer such public ridicule and humiliation.

Zsa Zsa Gabor, Rubirosa's flamboyant paramour, laughing at the wedding portrait of Barbara and "Rubi." Zsa Zsa sported an eye patch, claiming Rubirosa had given her a black eye because "he luffs *me*, dahlink!"

Looking almost unrecognizably plump, after the Rubirosa debacle Barbara married old friend Baron Gottfried Von Cramm, her "true love." She overlooked the implications of the fact that during the war the Baron had been arrested by the Nazis for homosexual acts.

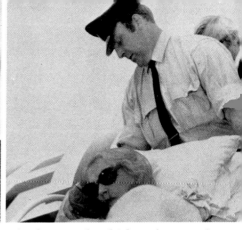

Barbara, looking older than her 53 years in this 1965 photograph, with her seventh husband. He was the gentle, soft-spoken Indonesian Prince Doan Vinh Na Champacak. He emerged $3 million richer.

A photograph which unfortunately typfies the Barbara Hutton of recent year No longer ambulatory, she is carried t and from her limousines and planes.

This beautiful blonde went relatively unnoticed in a 1940 Boston production of *Tobacco Road*. A few years later, as Winthrop Rockefeller's "Cinderella Bride," "Bobo" became world famous. Their separation and legal battles resulted in startling revelations about Rockefeller.

This filthy stairway in a tenement buil ing on New York's Third Avenue le to the elegant apartment occupied b "Bobo" while she was being courted b Winthrop.

The happy couple: "Bobo" and Winthrop Rockefeller, on their wedding day.

The Rockefellers with their friends, the socially prominent Winston Guests.

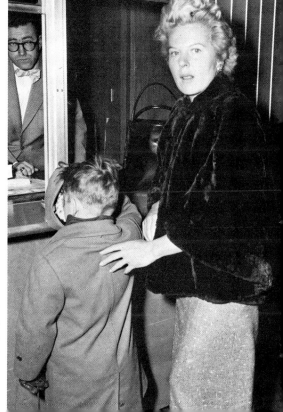

Long and bitter court battles with her husband concluded, "Bobo," enroute to Europe, refused to allow newsmen to photograph her son, Winthrop Rockefeller, Jr.

If one photograph can sum up Tommy Manville's life, this is it. His lust for the female form took him to the altar eleven times, cost him over three million dollars.

Manville always kept a revolver handy a his lavish Long Island home. "To kee his wives in line?" jested intimates.

An unusual threesome: Manville, Broadway producer Earl Carroll and Marcelle Edwards, one of Carroll's leading showgirls. She became Manville's fourth wife.

Bonita Edwards was Manville's fifth wif "She resembled Lana Turner," not Walter Winchell.

The sixth Mrs. Manville, Wilhelmina Connelly (Billy) Boze, looked like Betty Grable.

The world's one-and-only eight-hour bride: Macie Marie (Sunny) Ainsworth. She was #7.

Georgina Campbell was wife #8. A contemporary touch: the leather strap around her neck.

Anita Roddy-Eden, Mrs. Tommy Manville #9, being carried across the threshold by her ardent, aging groom. Except for dozens of newsmen and photographers, they were alone!

"I do!" said Tommy as he took his tenth bride, Pat Gaston, in 1957.

With Christina Erdlen, the eleventh—and last—Mrs. Tommy Manville.

Heir to the Seagram liquor fortune, Edgar Bronfman sued for annulment from his fair Lady Carolyn after a most incredible honeymoon and absolutely sex-less marriage.

immune to corruption. Martin T. Manton, Chief Judge of the United States District Court of the Southern District of New York, was convicted and sent to prison, as was Otto Kerner, former Governor of Illinois and Judge of the United States Court of Appeals in that state.

Corruption lies in the weakness of the man, and not of the judicial system or the jury system. A wrench thrown into a piece of machinery hardly indicates that the machinery is defective. It is the wrench throwers who are at fault—not the machinery.

It was ironic that Judge Mills was now hopeful of being the beneficiary of a jury aberration. Years before, when asked by a friend to explain how an almost unbelievable jury verdict had been arrived at in his Court, Judge Mills replied, "It was temporary insanity by twelve men who became sane immediately upon leaving the courtroom." He hoped the findings of the jury in the Rhinelander case would place Justice Morschauser in a position to give a similar explanation.

Davis was in the driver's seat, no doubt about that. He strongly felt that he had the case won, and his strategy from now on would be to play it safe. The only possible way to lose was to have Alice make a fool of herself on cross-examination. But there was an amazingly simple way to avoid this: Don't put her on as a witness! Judge Mills couldn't cross-examine an empty chair.

He would contend that being compelled to disrobe in the juryroom had so unnerved and upset Alice that she was now too ill to testify. Judge Mills might scream that Davis, in permitting Alice to disrobe in the juryroom, had actually called her as a witness. But if Davis claimed she was too ill to testify, Mills could yell his head off, and it would make no difference.

Davis would call Alice's sister Emily, their mother, and a doctor as witnesses. Then, after summations by the lawyers and the judge's charge, the case would go to the jury.

Had Davis been able to foresee the future, he would not have put Alice's mother on the witness stand.

Davis put Emily Jones on the stand, to show that Leonard had seen not only members of the Jones family who lived at home, and Grace, who lived in the house next door, but also one who lived away from the immediate neighborhood.

Emily testified that she met Leonard at her father's house many times, and young Rhinelander had often been a dinner guest at her home, over the garage at the household where her husband was employed. (Emily had married Robert Brooks, a butler for a family in Pelham, New York.)

She further testified that Leonard was on a first-name basis with her husband, who was very obviously black. They seemed to enjoy each other's company, and they played poker with her husband's friends, who were *all* black.

The cross-examination of Emily was very brief. Judge Mills saw little to gain from emphasizing Leonard's friendship with a black butler.

The next witness was Dr. Caesar P. McClendon, of New Rochelle, a black physician and a graduate of the medical school of the University of Michigan. He told of treating Alice for influenza in October 1922, at the Jones house, and of meeting Rhinelander there.

"Can you point out Mr. Rhinelander in this courtroom?" Davis asked Dr. McClendon.

"He is the gentleman sitting there," said McClendon, pointing to Leonard.

"For purposes of the record," said Davis, "I must ask if you are colored."

With an accent of pride, McClendon replied, "I am."

"In your examination of Alice did you notice the color of her body?"

"It was of dark complexion, approximately as dark as mine."

"That is all, Doctor. Thank you. Your witness, Judge Mills."

In cross-examination, when lawyers have a highly reputable witness whose testimony is simple, if they have reason to believe the testimony cannot be shaken or refuted, it is wise to get the witness off the stand as quickly as possible. To do otherwise would be to emphasize and magnify the testimony. Judge Mills did not cross-examine Dr. McClendon.

Davis now called his final witness. "Mrs. Elizabeth Jones, will you please take the witness stand."

Alice's mother, after being sworn, sat down. She was pathetically frail and tired, in some ways resembling a faded flower. The dusky color of the previous witness was in marked contrast to her pale face. She spoke with an English accent, in a voice so low that it barely reached the jury.

She testified that she had first met her husband, George Jones, at Bradford, England, while she was a cook on a large estate where Jones was the coachman. "We were married in Leeds, thirty-six years ago," she said, "and a little over a year later came to this country."

"You knew when you married Mr. Jones that he had colored blood?"

"Yes," she answered, but added that in England he was known as a mulatto, and there was no prejudice there against him because of his color.

"Did the name *Rhinelander* mean anything to you?" asked Davis, introducing the subject of Rhinelander's appearance in the Jones's home.

"No, the name meant nothing at all," she replied, and noted that after a while Rhinelander was at the house nearly every night and stayed over on weekends.

"Did you know about Alice's early-morning visits to Rhine‹ lander's room on those occasions?"

"I had no knowledge of it," she answered. "I don't think he was that kind of gentleman."

"Did you ever hear Mr. Rhinelander question your daughter's color?"

"No, never!"

"Mr. Rhinelander has said that in your presence Alice told him she was white."

"I never heard that spoken of," Mrs. Jones replied quietly.

Mrs. Jones further stated that Rhinelander had even shown her the wedding ring he had bought for Alice and asked her not to say anything about the marriage for a while. "But after the story about their marrying was all over the newspapers," said Mrs. Jones, "my husband told Mr. Rhinelander he objected to being called a Negro in the papers. My husband told Leonard, 'I am a colored man but not a Negro.' "

Mrs. Jones said Rhinelander also told her he would never deny marrying "the girl he had wanted and that he didn't care what anybody said or did."

Then she was asked about an alleged threat of the Ku Klux Klan, and replied, "Mr. Jacobs [Philip Rhinelander's lawyer] told me on one of his visits to my home that the Klan would kill me. Just before Mr. Jacob's visit someone had thrown three rocks through the windows of my house and that of my daughter Grace, who lives next door."

"That is all," Davis said gently, and turned Mrs. Jones over to Judge Mills for cross-cxamination.

Except for his upcoming summation to the jury, demolishing the credibility of this poignant witness represented Mills's last opportunity to affect the outcome of the case. He knew there would be little use in attacking the testimony Mrs. Jones had given—she would only repeat it. His only alternative was to attack her credibility and thus destroy her testimony. However, destroying her credibility would wind up the case on a high note for Mills.

Mills owed a duty to his client to use any legal means to protect his interests. If it involved flinging mud, he rationalized, Mrs. Jones had supplied the dirt.

In the 1920s the birth of an illegitimate child made a woman a social outcast. In light of today's mores, it is difficult to describe the scorn and humiliation then attendant upon such a personal catastrophe.

Currently honeymoons often are taken before marriage. The birth of children of unmarried mothers of prominence are items barely considered newsworthy. By 1975 no less prominent a personage than Mrs. Betty Ford, wife of the President of the United States, stated there seemed to be complete freedom in pre-marital sex, and it would not disturb her if her 18-year-old daughter had an affair. That school of thought seemed to set the tone in the 1970s.

But in the 1920s a woman who had an illegitimate child was a social leper, ostracized and shunned by friends and neighbors. To move to a different city, and sometimes another state, was a partial solution. To family and friends she was branded with a scarlet letter. Shame was her constant companion.

Philip Rhinelander had spent more than thirty thousand dollars investigating the background of the Jones family in England, and Judge Mills had on the counsel table investigative reports in a bound twenty-five-page folder. It contained the information with which he intended to destroy the credibility of the witness.

Judge Mills began by questioning Mrs. Jones about the manner of her meeting her husband, and his birthplace. She answered that her husband was born in Leicester, England. The estate where they had met and worked was called Huttoft, owned by a man named Turduff. The Turduff family consisted of an elderly man and a daughter who later married; Mrs. Jones couldn't recall their first names. She said she worked at the estate for a year before she left England with Jones to come to this country.

"Now, the shipping records show that Mr. Jones and you brought with you a child?" asked Mills.

"Yes, sir."

"A girl named Ethel?"

"Yes, sir."

"About six years old?"

"Yes, sir."

"How long were you married to Mr. Jones before you sailed from England?"

"About one month."

"This girl Ethel was entered on the shipping list as a Jones?"

"Yes."

"Was Mr. Jones the father of this child?" Mills asked slowly.

Davis sprang to his feet and exclaimed, "Judge, for heaven's sake, are you really going into this?"

"Yes, I am, Mr. Davis."

Davis was livid. "Thirty-five years ago! It happened thirty-five years ago!" he exclaimed. "Judge, this is monstrous!"

"Your Honor," said Mills, "I object to Mr. Davis's actions."

"I object to the question," Davis snapped angrily.

"That you have the right to do," replied Judge Mills. "I ask it on the question of credibility."

Justice Morschauser overruled Davis's objection. Mills repeated, "Was Mr. Jones the father of this child?"

Elizabeth Jones looked over at her attorney, her face totally drained of color. Davis could not help her. "You will have to answer it, Mrs. Jones," he said quietly.

Mrs. Jones sat in silence. Her face reflected the agonizing turmoil of an anguished mind, and she cringed at the stares of the spectators and jury. Her family sat by helplessly. Their eyes, filled with compassion and love, bridged the gap to attempt to comfort her.

"Was Mr. Jones her father?" Mills repeated relentlessly.

"No, sir," she said softly.

"Who was Ethel's father?"

"I object again!" Davis exclaimed angrily.

"Well, it goes to her credibility, Your Honor," said Mills, looking at Justice Morschauser.

Davis started to say, "Yes, but there must come a time, you know—" but he was interrupted by Justice Morschauser.

"I will overrule your objection, Mr. Davis. Judge Mills is within his legal rights."

"I shall go at it briefly," said Mills.

Davis would not give up. "I object to it as incompetent, immaterial, irrelevant, and absolutely unnecessary to any issue in this case," he stated heatedly.

"We will argue that when we sum up," retorted Mills.

"Gentlemen," interjected Justice Morschauser, pounding his gavel, "please desist from bickering and proceed."

"Who was the father of Ethel?" Mills asked again.

"I do not wish to answer it," Mrs. Jones replied faintly.

"You do not wish to answer it?"

"No, sir."

"Now she is within her legal rights," ruled Justice Mor-schauser. "You have the right to ask that question, Judge Mills, but the witness has the right to refuse to answer."

"Of course, Your Honor. I do not question that," said Mills. He then asked Mrs. Jones, "Were you married before you married George Jones?"

"I do not wish to answer that."

Mills turned to the Judge. "That I must insist upon, Your Honor."

"You will have to answer the question, Mrs. Jones," the Judge instructed her.

Mills repeated, "Were you married before you were married to George Jones?"

"I was not," replied Mrs. Jones, almost in a whisper.

Everyone in the courtroom was tense. The jurors were leaning forward, listening intently. Spectators were straining to catch her low tones. Emily and Grace Jones were squirming restlessly in their chairs, and Alice sat with her face in her hands. George Jones, his elbows resting on his knees, his face cupped in his hands, sat staring at his wife.

"Had you another child before Ethel was born?" continued Mills.

"No, sir."

"Didn't you have a child named William?"

"No, sir."

"Wasn't William brought up by your parents and is now living in this village of Huttoft?"

"No, sir."

At this point Davis jumped up. "Your Honor, I must object to this questioning as being repetitious and irrelevant."

"It is not irrelevant and is absolutely proper for the purpose of credibility," answered Mills.

"Your Honor, may we have a recess at this time?" asked Davis.

Justice Morschauser granted it at once.

After the Judge and jury had left the courtroom, Mrs. Jones sat down at the counsel table, surrounded by her daughters. She was in tears, sobbing softly. Her soul had been laid bare before her children, and the shame in her eyes was pitiful. Spectators stared sympathetically at her, many with lumps in their throats.

Mr. Jones, who had hurt his leg that morning, limped over to Judge Mills, who was talking animatedly with a friend. His voice trembling with anger, Jones said, "You lousy son of a bitch, why did you do it? Why did you have to do it?"

Mills, startled by the outburst, looked at Jones in disbelief and started to say something.

Davis quickly rushed over. "Mr. Jones, stop it! Stop it, please!"

But Jones, beside himself, looking as if he might strike Mills, kept repeating, "You lousy son of a bitch. Why did you have to do it?"

Davis again pleaded, "Please, please, stop it!" The last thing Davis wanted was Jones striking seventy-five-year-old Judge Mills. The sympathy sure to flow to Mills wouldn't do Alice's case any good.

Davis gently but firmly walked Jones out of the room and into the corridor. He stayed with him, smoking, for the duration of the recess, trying to calm and pacify him. To a friend who joined them he said, shaking his head slowly, "Judge Mills has reached a new high in stooping low."

The trial resumed fifteen minutes later. Whether because of the Jones outburst or because he felt it best to leave the matter with the jury at this point, Mills asked no further questions along this legal but ignoble line. After four innocuous questions came the welcome, "That is all."

The agony of the cross-examination of Mrs. Jones was ended. The testimony in the Rhinelander case was over.

After motions to be made by the lawyers, and the ruling on those motions by the judge, the attorneys would deliver their summations.

The attorney who makes the first opening statement makes the final closing statement, or summation. Generally, if the plaintiff has the "affirmative" of any issue raised by the pleadings, she or he has the right to open and close the case.

The guiding purpose in summation is to marshal the evidence into a persuasive argument to the jury. Counsel must keep within the record when referring to the facts of the case, and argument may not be made on facts about which the record is silent.

As a tactical matter, there is a substantial advantage in having the first and last word to a jury. A good opening can enlist the sympathetic interest of the jurors from the start; the final summation may often be the deciding factor in a case.

In summation, lawyers have appealed to reason, logic, prejudice, love, hate, fear—they have run the proverbial gamut of emotions. Summations are often dramatic efforts rivaling any ever seen in the theater. Some have reached true oratorical heights. Many would better have been left unuttered. Very often a summation is hours in length; not infrequently they have run into days.

Some lawyers seem to equate length with excellence. Samuel Untermeyer, one of the giants of the legal profession, said, "For a summation to be immortal it does not have to be eternal." Max D. Steuer, the best-known trial lawyer of his generation, quipped, "A summation should be like a woman's dress—long enough to cover the subject, but short enough to make it interesting." That seemed to sum it up.

Lee Parsons Davis walked slowly to the jury box and looked at the jurors with a soft sweep of his eyes, as if to establish a bond of understanding for what he was about to say.

He began his summation in a low key. Persons familiar with the Davis technique said he usually started that way. The fireworks, "the rocket's red glare, the bombs bursting in air," were sure to come.

Davis told the jury that the only thing he was really afraid of in the case was race prejudice. "If we cannot convince you by logical argument that the defendant should have your verdict, we should quit the practice of law. But there isn't an argument in the world that can batter successfully against the wall of race prejudice, because most of the people who are prejudiced still believe the earth is flat. How can you argue with them? We hate some people because we do not know them, and we will not know them because we hate them. It is a vicious circle. That is why we asked you, and ask you again, to be fair."

Davis then turned his attention to Judge Mills and warned the jury that although the Judge was elderly and bland he was "cute as a fox." He said he fully expected to object to Judge Mills during Mills's summation because of what he expected him to say, and he anticipated Mills would exclaim, "I didn't interrupt *you!*"

"Judge Mills will endeavor to put me in the position of an ingrate," said Davis, "because the judge has said that he started me in the practice of law. But the truth of the matter is that Judge Mills had nothing to do with my career, except that he was the only judge in Westchester County who opposed my appointment as district attorney. That's ingratitude, isn't it?" asked Davis, smiling.

He then continued in a louder voice, "We have rested this case without calling Alice Rhinelander or her father, Mr. Jones. Why is this?" His voice now vibrated with feeling. "We are determined that this girl shall no longer be dragged in the mire of slander which this man Jacobs, Judge Mills's associate, has gathered together and which he has theatened to use in an effort to tear to pieces what little reputation this poor girl still possesses. We have the right not to subject this poor girl to any more cruelty than has been heaped upon her. She has been dragged in the sewer and filth for weeks, and we will no longer permit them to do it.

"There was only one reason to call Alice Rhinelander to the stand," he continued, "and that was to deny something she has already denied. There is only one issue in the case—did Alice Rhinelander deceive her husband as to her color? Did she say, 'I am white'?

"That has already been denied by her mother. Her mother! Is there any man who can disbelieve this pure little woman, after the sacrifices she has made for her daughter? Any woman who would bare her life wouldn't lie to you on the witness stand. She was dragged through the mud, and she told the truth. She has shed countless tears on countless nights at the memory of a far-gone day, and Judge Mills dragged her through the slime to revive that memory so that she could again shed tears on more countless nights."

Davis now had a sob in his voice. "Is there no limit to the torture of this poor woman? Has she not suffered enough? Has Judge Mills no mercy?"

Davis was now savage in attacking the manner in which the case had been conducted and the sort of testimony that had been given. He charged Mills with attempting to wreck the reputation of everyone connected with the defense and said, "For shame on Judge Mills that he has read into the record this morning the fact that Ross Chidcster [the chauffeur] had been forced to pay for the support of an illegitimate child in New York. He could not attack the testimony that Chidester gave, because it is true, and he knows it is true. So he attacks him personally. For shame! For shame!"

Davis then hammered at the conduct of Leon R. Jacobs, the Rhinelander attorney of record, who, he said, was the "evil genius behind the case." He asked, "Why has not Philip Rhinelander been brought to court?" It was absurd to believe, he said, after young Rhinelander had been found at the Marie Antoinette by his father's attorney, that the Rhinelander family did not know Alice Jones was black.

"I am the only one to stand between this young girl and absolute ruin," declared Davis. "They have torn from her ruthlessly every scrap of respectability that a woman loves most. There isn't another thing they can do to this girl except one, and that would be for you to add the last straw and say, 'Alice Rhinelander, you must go out into the world as a fraud.' My failure here may result in absolute ruin to her."

Alice had taken her seat at the counsel table in front of the jury box, and for more than an hour during her attorney's impassioned appeals she sat with her face concealed, her shoulders shaking convulsively. She made no sound, however, and after a time her mother succeeded in soothing her so that she lifted her face, and sat silently and stolidly, as before.

Davis was now firing all batteries. He had already been talking for three hours. "Where was this young man Rhinelander when the trial started at ten o'clock on the opening day? He did not appear until two-thirty in the afternoon. Why? Let me tell you why. Jacobs kept him away because he did not want to have him hear Judge Mills in his opening statement brand him as 'brain-tied' and a 'boob.'

"Mr. Jacobs assured the court that this young man was on the way, but he kept him away until after Judge Mill's opening so that he would not hear it. If a member of the bar will deceive the Court on that matter, what will he not do when he gets down to the vitals of this case? In a case based on fraud the attorney of record was the first one to practice it. Judge Mills's opening was cruel. Mr. Jacobs knew this boy would not stand for that. He is tongue tied, but he is not brain-tied. Who's really back of this lawsuit that they didn't want their own client to hear the opening? Gentlemen of the jury, draw your own conclusions."

Davis then took up the question of the manner in which he had introduced the two "mystery" letters. "Who protested against the filth in this case? Who cautioned that if they started it we would see the fight through? Would you have us sit here and watch them drag this girl in the sewer? Never! Never! Never!" he exclaimed in rising crescendo.

"They wanted to throw slime and see what its reaction would be on twelve men. As an attorney at the bar I am opposed to trying cases like this in public. I am not criticizing the newspapers for publishing it when it is offered to them, but I would never let them have a chance at it. This case should never have been tried before the world, because we do not know what terrible effect it may have on the youth not only of this country but of the entire world.

"The death of Leonard Rhinelander's mother, who died in a fire when he was young, was a terrible thing. But I don't know whether death by burning is to be preferred to the living death which Judge Mills has brought to this old woman!"

Davis paused for a moment and then dramatically turned to point to Mrs. Jones. "I'd rather be burned at the stake than as a seventy-five-year-old man stand before a woman like Mrs. Jones and tear from her the secret of her eighteen-year-old girlhood. That is a living death.

"Many a white heart beats under a dark skin," continued Davis, turning his attention now to Mr. Jones. "This little woman stuck to him. He kept her secret. For thirty-five years they lived happily together. My God! How can the Rhinelanders ever forgive themselves? They allowed their senior counsel to disgrace this mother, to disgrace this daughter, and for what? For nothing! I haven't been practicing fifty years at the bar as Judge Mills has, but I wouldn't have dragged that out of this woman if there had been a millon dollars at stake. Not for all the money in the world!"

Davis seemed deeply moved as he was concluding his long appeal to the jury. He had been speaking for more than six hours. His voice was deep and husky from his efforts, and his eyes were filled with tears as he came to the final moments. He leaned over toward the jury box and again begged the jury to guard against race prejudice. "There is no possibility of the Rhinelanders' living together again after what was said at this trial. Please do not concern yourselves with that. They will never live together. You have now only to decide whether this marriage is to be declared the result of a fraud. Let them weep no more. They have wept too much. They have suffered too much. Too much. Too much."

The courtroom was absolutely quiet. Davis had delivered a brilliant, heart-rending appeal. The jurors were emotionally drained, and so were many of the spectators.

Judge Mills, who had received a personal pounding many times during the six hours, came over to Davis and, in full view of everyone, shook his hand and said, "That was great, Lee. Simply great!" Some of the jurors and spectators were startled at the scene. The "old fox" had justified his reputation. By going over and making a sportsmanlike show of shaking hands, he had taken some of the sting out of Davis's lashes. He had broken part of Davis's spell.

Judge Mills began his summation with a blatant appeal to race prejudice: "You might as well bury this young man six feet deep in the soil of the old churchyard where his early American ancestors sleep as to condemn him to be chained for eternity to this mulatto woman," he said. No kleagle of the Ku Klux Klan had ever been more specific.

"There is not a father among you who would not rather

see his son dead than wedded to this colored woman. There is room in this fair country for blacks as well as whites, but the decent blacks object to this marriage as much as decent whites."

Mills then traced the early education of Leonard Rhinelander, who, he said, "was no ornament to society, that's plain to see." He pictured Leonard at the time he first met Alice Jones as having the normal intelligence of a fourteen-year-old boy. Mills thundered that Alice had sexually enslaved young Rhinelander, made him abject in his fear of losing her, and played on his emotions until he literally did not know black from white.

Again and again he returned to his theme of racial prejudice. "There is not a mother in this land who would not rather see her daughter with her hands crossed above her shroud than locked in the embrace of a mulatto man. That is the issue. Great heavens! What can life itself hold for this young man with that face of inexpressible sadness if he is to remain chained to her? Look at him! He looks thirty years old. There have been witticisms in this case, but he has never smiled. He will hail your verdict, if you find a verdict for him, as a person on the steps of the scaffold welcomes a reprieve from the governor."

Mills then again appealed to the jury to look at the race issue, but then, in a burst of eloquence, he said, "We must take the bull by the tail and look the situation squarely in the face."

The malapropism brought gales of laughter from jury and spectators. Even Justice Morschauser found difficulty refraining from laughing, but Lee Parsons Davis attempted no restraint: "Judge, you meant take the bull by the horns, didn't you?" laughed Davis.

"Yes, I did," said the unflappable Mills. "That's what comes from not being brought up on a farm."

Undaunted, Mills then made the most of every artifice he had learned in his years at the bar. He smilingly refused to exhibit those oratorical gestures of which Davis had warned the jury the day before. But sometimes in the warmth of his delivery he raised a clenched fist above his white head and shook it as his voice vibrated with a true actor's tremor.

Mill's gestures and voice were moderated carefully. He made reference to George Washington, Abraham Lincoln, and Theodore Roosevelt. He was really waving the flag. As he spoke one could almost hear drums beating and bugles blowing. Spectators half-expected Mills to reenact a scene charging up San Juan Hill with the Rough Riders.

Through it all Alice gazed at the picturesque elderly figure before her as if fascinated. Part of the time she sat with a finger between her lips, biting it slowly, or twisting her fingers in her lap and peering up from under the brim of her hat. She had the attitude of one disinterestedly watching a drama. Her mother and father seemed more distraught.

Davis sat between Alice and the jury box, occasionally resting his head on a hand under his chin, with his elbow on the counsel table. His eyes were closed, as if glad of the opportunity to relax after the strain of his own summation.

"This boy loved his wife and believed everything she told him," continued Mills. "That is the sad part of this case. He was struck insensate by the news that she was not white. He urged her to make a frank statement to reporters, and she did so, denying that she was black. He believed her then.

"Why, when he returned from his trip he went to her before he sought his father's home. When she threatened to throw him out he pleaded with her not to, as he might plead to the daughter of a queen. Of course, she had no thought of throwing him out. He was dead in love with her. He loved her until his lawyers brought the birth records—do you blame him for then not loving her any longer?

"I seek no fame by injuring a woman though that woman be of the basest kind," said Mills scornfully. "I'd expect my sainted mother to rise from her grave and strike me down if I dared it. I do not believe in divorce, for I was taught to believe that whom heaven has joined together no man should put asunder. I hold that the interests of the public would be better served if there were no divorce. But there can be no prejudice against the annulment of an alliance which was void from its inception because of the fraud."

Mills mentioned thankfully that there were no children of the marriage. He said that the couple could never live together again and that Alice would gain rather than lose by the annulment.

"After that indecent exhibition in the juryroom, she shed tears," he continued, pointing to Alice, whom he never once referred to as *Mrs. Rhinelander* during the trial. "And they were genuine tears, for what woman would not weep after such a thing? But with the buoyancy of her race she will regain her spirits. She will rally when the scandal passes. Let her gain a husband of her own race and find happiness with him as did her sister Emily, who without vaulting ambition wed within her own color and kind."

Next to feel the fist of Mill's stinging rhetoric was Alice's mother. Judge Mills pictured Mrs. Jones as eagerly seeking white husbands for her daughters, as being willing to accept any young man who came to her home in her pursuit for white men. Mills thundered that the Joneses "went to a white church and a white Sunday school, and the daughters sought white men on the streets of New Rochelle and brought them home, where the mother received them without asking their names."

Mills then answered Davis's objections to his having brought into the case the Marie Antoinette episode and the girl's letters. "Why, if we had not done this the case would have gone out of the door," said Mills, his voice rising. "If this were not done there would be no remedy for our youth taken into a marriage by fraud. There would be no basis for fraud charges in the annulment of marriages. Not to have done that would notify every vampire that she may follow her trade without fear of consequences."

Mills justified bringing in the letters because the answer filed by the defense when the trial opened had denied that Alice had "colored" blood. After the trial started this answer was amended to admit the "colored" blood, and Mills said this showed that after the case opened Davis knew his client had deceived him.

Davis angrily jumped to his feet. "Is there any evidence that she deceived me?" he demanded.

After some argument between Mills and Davis, Justice Morschauser pointed out to the lawyers that both sides had amended their papers, so that they could start even from that point.

Judge Mills went on to say that Davis should have known from this circumstance that "Alice's defense was utterly hopeless. If Mr. Davis had frankly admitted the deception there would have been no necessity to introduce the letters to make the long chain of evidence to prove fraud. I hurl back, therefore, that it is *he* that is responsible for the publication of those letters throughout the length and breadth of the land."

"What are you doing, charging that I should have laid down in this case?" Davis asked sarcastically.

"Yes, if you came to those conclusions," answered Mills. "Otherwise I have no criticism to make of your conduct."

Mills forged ahead. He went exhaustively into Davis's cross-examination of Rhinelander regarding Leonard's motives in writing the "mystery" letters. He discussed them very frankly, including all the incidents surrounding the trip to the Marie Antoinette and the stay there. In Mill's view the letters showed that Rhinelander had been reduced to the depths of degradation, enslaved by his future wife.

"How could any man, making the advances he made, believe the girl to be innocent?" he asked, as he stared directly at Alice.

Judge Mills then turned to the question of his examination of Mrs. Jones. "I threw no rocks at her," he said. There was sarcastic laughter from the audience, which Justice Morschauser quickly stopped.

"The reason I have brought out the facts," Mills went on, "was that when confronted by the denial of color on Alice's part I deemed it necessary to call the illegitimate daughter as a witness, and it was essential to establish her identity. The blame rests on Mr. Davis in not making known earlier that he would withdraw the claim that Alice was not colored, and not on me."

He then paid his respects to Davis for giving warning that the case was stirring up violent emotions, adding, "I have no guard beside me, despite the fact that I've received threatening letters."

Davis jumped to his feet to protest that that wasn't in the evidence, and Mills "apologetically" withdrew his remark.

He then referred to Davis's repudiation of the Mills protection and tutelage and commented, "He repudiates me! While taking notes during his summation I said to myself, 'Thank heaven I never taught law to that man. It would be a bad reflection on me.' I might have had some thought of retiring four weeks ago when this case started, but although I have not taken that new gland treatment [a treatment then in vogue, using monkey glands for rejuvenation], I have taken four weeks of Davis's foolish arguments, and now I know I'm

still good, and good for ten more years of successful practicing."

Judge Mills accounted for Alice's admission to her husband
before their marriage that she had been intimate with another
man by saying that she must have done it "to impress Leonard Rhinelander with the sacrifice she was making in giving
up this other man for him. What a sacrifice!" he observed
sarcastically.

Mills then demanded to know why Mr. Jones had not
taken the stand to deny the Englishman-with-the-jaundice
remark. Finally he concluded for the day, stating that he was
almost through answering Davis's charges and that he would
complete his summing up tomorrow.

Davis, standing up from the counsel table and gathering
together his papers, smilingly remarked to Mills, "You spent
most of your time on my trivialities, didn't you, Judge?"

"I have, I have," Mills retorted blandly. "But there was
nothing else to spend time on."

The next day Mills called on ancient and biblical history
to prove that there could be differing versions of the same
story. He quoted Matthew, Mark, Luke, and John to show
how accounts by different persons of the same events vary.
"History is full of such chronicles. In Holy Writ it is told
how Samson, that great leader of his people, was beguiled
by a woman, and when he lay with his head in her lap she cut
cut off his locks and made him powerless."

"Did they annul that marriage?" inquired Davis facetiously,
interrupting Mills's dramatic diatribe.

"Will Your Honor instruct counsel not to interrupt?" demanded Mills. Justice Morschauser looked disapprovingly at
Davis.

Mills went on. With a quivering voice, he retold the story

of Salome and John the Baptist and how the evil mother—
"there is always an evil mother!" he exclaimed—told Salome
to beg for John's head.

Then: "The greatest war of ancient times was fought over
a woman," intoned Mills, and with lifted arms he paid tribute
to Homer and Helen of Troy. He brought in Cleopatra and
Marc Antony, then quickly passed over the centuries to Lord
Nelson, Lady Hamilton, Trafalgar, and the glories of the British Empire.

Davis rose at this point to voice a mild reproof over the
judge's excursion backward in time, which was "seeming to
run far afield. It is a nice lesson in history, but it has nothing
to do with this case."

Mills told Davis, "Be patient. Everything will fall into
place."

"We should all live that long," replied Davis, smiling.

Judge Mills continued. Almost without pausing to take a
deep breath he turned from ancient history to modern times.
"Many a great man has fallen and become the abject slave of
some chorus girl who could not write a sentence of English.
This power woman has over us is a tremendous thing. When
it is exercised for good it is an inspiration, but when it is exercised for bad it is a degrading influence."

Next in Mills's verbal spotlight were the Scopes trial
(the so-called "monkey trial") and Jonah and the whale,
with which he intended to prove his point about the
doubts existing in Leonard's mind regarding Alice's color.
"You have read of Clarence Darrow and the cross-
examination of Bryan at the great trial we had down in
Tennessee," intoned Mills. "Remember when Darrow asked
Bryan if he believed that the whale had swallowed
Jonah? Had I been on the witness stand I would have had to

answer that I had some doubt but that I would stick by my guns in my belief of the Bible.

"What is my point? It is that this young man still believed in his wife, although doubts had been raised in his mind, the same way that doubts are raised in the minds of many about Jonah and the whale. Are you going to condemn a man who still believed in his wife in the face of slanders and reports appearing in the newspapers?"

Mills then read a letter of Rhinelander's to prove that Leonard loved his wife and that he was her slave. After a few more remarks Mills said, "I am at an end. I have given this case the best that is in me. The responsibility now passes to you. Your verdict will answer once more the question in Holy Writ, 'Can the Ethiopian change the color of his skin?' Your answer must be in the negative. No, it can't be done.

"This case has not been without difficulties. It is hard to stand here and speak of these people without restraint. You should have no hesitation in giving this young man a chance to live, a change to redeem himself. I am through. I leave this young man, twenty-two years old, in your hands. Relieve him from this horrid, unnatural, absurd, and terrible union. I pray you to grant him deliverance."

The summations were over. Spectators had been emotionally drained, first by Davis and now by Judge Mills. For hours they had listened, sometimes in anger, often in disagreement, but always with intense interest.

Davis had taken six hours; Mills, nine. Mills had exercised to the fullest the wide latitude permitted in summation. He had stepped out of bounds on more than one occasion. He was blatantly racist and had appealed to the basest prejudices. But overall he had made an effective appeal for his client.

Justice Morschauser asked the jurors, "Do you wish to consider the case tonight or tomorrow morning?" After a brief consultation the jurors requested that it go over to the next day, and the judge announced he would read his charge to the jury the first thing in the morning.

A Judge's charge is the Court's instructions on the principles of law governing the case. Although the Court may recapitulate the evidence, to coordinate and clarify the proof with respect to the issues, it must not encroach upon the province of the jury as the trier of the facts.

Justice Morschauser had a well-earned reputation for the clarity and fairness of his charges to juries.

The next day, the Judge read his charge. He reviewed the evidence in the case and hurried over some of the unsavory testimony as if he disliked to recall it. He then said, "The defendant did not offer herself as a witness. She did not call her father as a witness. Well, you might say, her father was in court, and was as available to Mr. Rhinelander as to her, and that Mr. Rhinelander could have called both his wife and her father if he chose.

"But on the other hand, you could say, 'Why should the plaintiff call them and take any chances on how they would testify when he had what he deemed sufficient evidence?' He could assume that they would testify against him.

"Mr. Davis for the defendant presented reasons why he did not call her and commented upon the fact that the father of the plaintiff was not called by the plaintiff.

"Judge Mills, for the plaintiff, commented upon and criticized the failure to call the defendant and her father as witnesses and asked you to draw unfavorable inferences therefrom, that it could be assumed the plaintiff's case would have been aided had either one of them taken the stand.

"While no presumption arises in this respect you are at

liberty and can give it such consideration and draw such inferences as you think are warranted by the proof from the failure to call such witnesses or to call any witness who might shed any light upon the case. Except in certain specific instances and then under specific circumstances there is generally no hard-and-fast rule that uniformly applies.

"Neither the defendant nor the plaintiff is bound to call every person as a witness who might give some material evidence in his or her favor; and yet, if they do not, you are at liberty to deem it of sufficient importance to merit your consideration."

Justice Morschauser paused to sip some water, then continued, "Gentlemen, you will always come to the question of what you believe to be true, after you weigh the testimony with the probabilities and consider the fair and reasonable inferences which you draw from the established facts. . . .

"You are the sole judges of the facts. You are the truth finders. The plaintiff bears the burden of proof to establish by a fair preponderance of proof the charges he made against the defendant. If he fails in this, you must answer the questions accordingly."

Justice Morschauser then went into a summary of the testimony of the plaintiff and the witnesses for the defendant regarding the facts and circumstances the jury could consider in determining whether Rhinelander had known that Alice was of "colored" blood.

"Now then, gentlemen," concluded the Judge, "in the final determination of this case by you, if you allow yourselves to be influenced by your sympathy, or prejudice, you do the parties an injustice. Sentiment, passion, and prejudice, or other influences should not interfere with honest determinations. An honest, courageous determination upon the evidence is required of you by your oaths."

At 12:30 P.M. the twelve men were in the juryroom. Slowly the foreman read aloud the seven questions of fact they would have to decide:

1. At the time of the marriage of the parties was the defendant colored and of colored blood?
2. Did the defendant before the marriage by silence conceal from the plaintiff the fact she was of colored blood?
3. Did the defendant before the marriage represent to the plaintiff that she was not of colored blood?
4. Did the defendant practice said concealment or make said representation with the intent thereby to induce the plaintiff to marry her?
5. Was the plaintiff by said concealment or by said representation, or both, induced to marry the defendant?
6. If the plaintiff had known that the defendant was of colored blood, would he have married her?
7. Did the plaintiff cohabit with the defendant after he obtained full knowledge that the defendant was of colored blood?

Justice Morschauser would make his decision on the basis of the jury's replies to these questions.

After the jury left the courtroom to deliberate, Davis and the Jones family went to his office, across the street from the courthouse. It would undoubtedly be hours before the jury could reasonably be expected to arrive at any conclusions, and Davis advised the Joneses to relax.

During the afternoon people who were able to get near the juryroom could hear heated, loud "discussions," indicating that considerable wrangling was going on within the room.

At 6:00 P.M., when no verdict had yet been reached, Justice Morschauser, with Davis and Mills present, ordered the jury to continue their deliberations, with instructions that if they could unanimously come to a conclusion on the seven questions during the next four hours they were to seal their findings in an envelope and hand it to the clerk of the court. The judge would receive it the following morning at ten.

When the jury retired, a fatigued Justice Morschauser left for a hotel near the courthouse. Davis returned to his office and informed the Jones family, "Go home, try not to worry, and be back in the courtroom at 10:00 A.M. tomorrow."

In his expressions to Alice and her family Davis had been cautiously confident that the jury's findings would be in her favor. In prognostications to his associates, however, he was highly optimistic, "more certain of the result than in any case I have ever tried."

But he cautioned all concerned not to go overboard in their optimism: "You never can tell what a jury will do."

Alice, hopeful about the outcome, was nonetheless depressed. Although she felt almost certain she would win, she also knew her dream was over—not because of anything she had or hadn't said or anything she had or hadn't done; not even because she was "good" or "bad," rich or poor. It was because she was "colored."

For Alice, life since childhood had been one of extreme poverty, made livable only by continuous fantasizing about hopes of what the future would bring. She often daydreamed of living in a nice home with fine clothes and a car, of trips to foreign lands where people danced and played, with plenty to eat. Always with plenty to eat. Although the Jones family did not starve when Alice was young, food wasn't free, and when money was in short supply—a frequent situation for the Joneses—food was none too plentiful.

Alice had had to work since she was thirteen to help support the family, and her jobs had been mostly in laundries. The job at the New York Athletic Club paid only six dollars a week, but it included two meals a day, and that was important. Very important.

When she met Leonard in 1921, Alice was working as a chambermaid in a hotel. Meeting him was a dream come true. His free spending and evident wealth opened whole new worlds to Alice. When Rhinelander gave her the key to his Stutz Bearcat, she gave him the key to her heart.

If Alice was disappointed that Leonard was no all-American football hero in appearance and no spellbinding orator, he possessed compensatory features that made it simple to overlook his defects. And he did, after all, love her for herself, and that was tremendously important to Alice and her ego. Just as Leonard had closed his eyes to many things in his infatuation for Alice, she had done the same for him. They both saw what they wanted to see, and each was happy in what the other had to offer.

Now, regardless of the outcome of the trial, the feelings between them were irrevocably damaged. Alice had appealed to Leonard as no other girl had. He had met many ambitious females in his social circle who would have encouraged a romance for the sake of the Rhinelander social position and wealth. Alice had done nothing more or less than many of her white counterparts would have done had they been given the opportunity. And Alice's mother had done nothing more or less than mothers in the Rhinelander social sphere would have done to encourage their daughters to latch on to the Rhinelander name.

Up until the trial Alice had believed that Leonard still

loved her and would not leave her. She felt his father had forced him to instigate the case. She had felt that Leonard would go along up to a point and then balk. Until it happened, Alice could not believe that her husband would ever really take the witness stand. Why would his father's wishes prevail any more than they had when he sent Leonard on a six-month cruise to break up their romance?

She had recalled to Davis, with a catch in her throat, that when Leonard came back, he had said, "Nothing will ever keep us apart. Nothing!" He had meant it, since three days later they were married.

When Leonard had been late on the first day of the trial (because his lawyer did not want to have him hear himself characterized as a boob and brain-tied), Alice had joyfully thought he wasn't there because he would not go through with the case. She felt almost a physical blow when he walked into the courtroom. It was a numbing shock when he took the witness stand and forever shattered her dreams.

Awaiting the verdict, Judge Mills, because of his age and physical condition, went to rest for a few hours in the judge's chambers, at Justice Morschauser's suggestion. Mills was very tired and in no mood for conversation. When a close friend, Frank Dorman, came in to offer good wishes and to say a few words about the case, Mills interrupted him: "Frank, will you please be sure that anything you are going to say will be an improvement on silence!" Mills was obviously in low spirits.

Leonard, meanwhile, was doing some reflecting on his own. In his room at the Gramatan Inn in Bronxville, he restlessly paced back and forth, biting his fingernails. His attorney, Leon Jacobs, dressed in his usual morning coat, striped pants, and spats, had gone down to the dining room for dinner. Leonard had no appetite and had refused Jacob's plea to come down and "just have coffee."

Leonard Rhinelander had no hopes of winning the case. He hadn't had any since he testified and realized how difficult it would be for any group of halfway intelligent people, after seeing Alice and her family, to believe he had not known Alice's color.

Yet up to a point, it hadn't made any difference to him. He had loved Alice, and it really had not mattered to him what she was. As a writer of the day commented, "To Leonard the bluebird of happiness could come in any color. Yes, the bluebird could even be black."

Leonard was amazingly free of race prejudice. He was quite aware that his family and many of his friends looked down on practically everyone—Irish, Jews, Italians, Orientals, blacks. This was especially true of his father. Rhinelander, Sr., hardly discriminated on the basis of wealth, for there were Jewish bankers and industrialists as wealthy as Philip Rhinelander with whom he wouldn't associate.

The only exception was the Rothschilds, but only because there had been a business relationship between the Rothschilds and the Rhinelanders for more than a century, and Philip was maintaining a tradition. Rhinelander was a great believer in tradition. To him, no one existed as a Rhinelander peer except WASPS—*wealthy* White Anglo-Saxon Protestants.

If Leonard had had no physical shortcomings he probably would have been no different in his outlook than his father. But the cruelty that children show each other in emphasizing defects had made Leonard tolerant of people. Consequently he had grown up almost untainted by prejudice. He despised no one, hated no one, and had no "anti" feelings about anyone. When he met Alice he had few prejudices to overcome.

But as a result of the pretrial events Leonard did change. After his father and Jacobs pounded, and pounded, and pounded, the poison of racism was injected into Leonard. And now he was not brain-tied, as Mills contended; he was brain-washed.

He had taken the first step when he consented to institute the annulment proceeding. The next was getting up on the witness stand and stating the series of denials and affirmations that led to his complete repudiation of Alice. He had crossed his Rubicon. There was no turning back.

It was bitter irony that only when he committed a social blunder had Leonard's family taken an interest in him. While he was away at the Orchard School, neither his father nor other members of the family came to visit him. They didn't seem to care particularly whether he was living or dead or how miserable he was. He was treated as the misfit of the family—someone to be hidden from view.

But now, because of his gargantuan "social faux-pas," there was a sudden interest in his life. And Leonard's family were not the only ones who were suddenly concerned with his actions. Many of Philip Rhinelander's peers were upset that Leonard's testimony about his liaisons at the Marie Antoinette and making love in his automobile were a bad example for their sons and daughters. What hypocrisy! What a laugh! Leonard was furious. If the parents could see their sons and daughters guzzling bootleg liquor in speakeasies and what went on at weekend parties in college towns, they would realize that their innocent lambs had little to learn from him. Most of them were postgraduate students of the jazz age; the Rhinelander scion was only a freshman.

Leonard felt positive he would lose the annulment proceeding, and Alice would still legally be his wife. But he knew there was no going back to her—they could never live together again.

And all because a woman had a dark skin. Where was the logic of it? Because Alice was part black they called her black. By the same reasoning wasn't she part white? Then why not call her white? She was more white than black. Her mother was completely white, and her father was only half-black, which meant Alice had three white grandparents and only one black!

Where would Leonard go from here? He assumed Judge Mills and Jacobs would have solutions to his problems, for part of the problem was legal. And his father would have an answer. He always did.

The jury came to a unanimous decision at eleven that evening. They handed their findings to the clerk of the court, who had been instructed by Justice Morschauser to remain as long as the jury did. The Clerk placed the sealed envelope in his safe.

As the jurors filed from the courtroom past a group of newsmen and some others who had been patiently waiting, one reporter called out, "Is it all over?"

"Yes, it's all over and sealed," answered one of the jurors, as he continued on into the street with his companions. A short time after the jurors had departed, the courthouse was locked.

The following morning the courtroom was packed, and excitement permeated the gathered throng. There seemed no doubt in anyone's mind about the verdict. So much so that people were certain there had been a leak from one of the jurors or the Clerk of the Court to whom the envelope had been given. Since it was virtually impossible to believe the Clerk would have opened a sealed envelope, it was deduced the information had definitely trickled from a juror. Rumors of the jury's alleged findings spread like wildfire.

Outside it was dark and gloomy, with an icy rain beating

steadily against the windowpanes. The courtroom lights had been turned on.

Justice Morschauser entered the courtroom promptly at 10, to the now familiar "All rise." When the jurors filed in, some of them were wearing overcoats, as if anxious to leave as soon as possible after their long and tiresome task.

The Judge warned the spectators that there must be no outbursts when the verdict was announced. "This is not a circus," he cautioned. "There must be no demonstration."

He asked the foreman of the jury, Clarence H. Pietsch, whether the seven questions had been answered.

"They have, Your Honor."

After opening the sealed envelope and perusing the contents the judge asked Davis and Mills, "Shall I read the answers, gentlemen?"

They both nodded.

As the judge read the findings there were hushed gasps among the spectators—each and every answer was in favor of Alice.

A sallow-faced Judge Mills requested that the jury be polled. The questions and answers were read to each juror, who was then asked if that was his answer. Each confirmation was duly noted by the court stenographer. After the last of the jurors had answered, a quietly exultant Lee Davis said, "May I on behalf of the defense express my appreciation and thanks to the jury."

Justice Morschauser thanked the jury for their long and patient service. Then with the quiet humor that had made him one of the most popular jurists in Westchester County, he said, "I will have you relieved from further jury duty for one year unless you wish to serve." The jurors laughed, practically in unison, and with almost one voice replied, "No thanks!"

Judge Mills then made a request to be heard on a motion

to dismiss the findings of the jury as "contrary to the evidence."

Under the law of this case the jury was acting as an advisory body to the Court regarding the facts, but the final decision rested with the Judge. He could set aside their findings if he wished, and Mills had to make the motion so that the record would be clear for an appeal in the event the motion was denied.

"I am not here to give my views as to how the jury was misled," stated Mills, "but it is obvious they gave their answers without any intelligent comprehension of the questions. They simply answered them in the manner which they thought would produce the result they desired."

Justice Morschauser requested both sides to submit briefs on the question. At the end of ten days he denied the motion, and a later motion for a retrial was also denied. On appeals to the Appellate Division, and later to the Court of Appeals, Justice Morschauser's dismissal of the complaint of Leonard Kip Rhinelander for an annulment of his marriage to Alice Jones Rhinelander was upheld.

A radiant Alice, smiling through her tears, left the courtroom after the jury's findings. Her depression of the previous night had understandably vanished. Now highly elated, she told Davis, "I feel like I'm on a cloud."

After the verdict Davis had said, "There was one danger facing my client that I was really worried about—race prejudice. It is most gratifying to be reassured that the jurors of Westchester County, at least, can rise above passions and prejudices and decide cases upon the facts and the law."

Newspaper reporters interviewing several jurors after the verdict confirmed that Davis was right in his conclusions.

Members of the jury had all agreed soon after they began

their deliberations that they could give only one verdict on the facts as presented to them. "We very early made up our minds as to how the case should be decided," said Clarence Pietsch, the jury foreman. "We took up the questions one at a time, and the number of the questions delayed us somewhat. The only question which gave us any trouble, however, was the sixth, as to whether he would have married her had he known she was colored.

"Race prejudice didn't enter into the case at all, and neither did the unsavory details in the letters. We decided it merely as a case between a man and a woman, and in reaching our verdict considered Rhinelander as a normal man with normal senses of perception. We didn't consider what the future might hold for them, as that was not up to us for decision."

Juror William J. Demarest, of Rye, standing with several of his fellow jurors, confirmed this: "We want it clearly understood that not for a single instant did race prejudice enter into consideration of our verdict. That was gratifying to all of us. We considered and discussed the evidence presented in court, and the evidence alone. The fact that we had to argue so long was due to discrepancies in our understanding of certain parts of the testimony. Every doubt in our minds was dissolved, before we affixed our signatures to the verdict."

There was, however, some sympathy for Rhinelander, as shown by the comment of juror Henry M. Well of Elmsford, who said, "If we had voted according to our hearts the verdict might have been different. But we voted in accordance with the evidence."

About three weeks after the trial ended Davis happened to meet Judge Mills in the lobby of the Astor Hotel, on Broadway, in New York. They greeted each other warmly, and

Davis invited Mills and Mills's friend Oscar Harwood for drinks in the Astor bar. To Davis's surprise, Mills accepted.

"Judge, it's nice to see you without worrying about how you intend to harpoon me," laughed Davis, after they were seated.

"Well, Lee, I suppose I was more worried about your harpoons than you were about mine."

"Not really, Judge. But there is one thing that has been bothering me, and I would like to ask you about it. May I?"

"Go right ahead," replied a curious Mills.

"Judge, I've known you for a long time, and I never believed you to be a racist. But some of the statements you made at the trial made you sound like a red-hot Mississippi politician. I can't believe you really feel that way. Do you?"

Mills sipped some red wine. "My friend Oscar here knows my feelings on the subject—we've had many arguments over it. If you're talking about mixed marriages, Lee, I do. And there's nothing wrong about the way I feel. Abraham Lincoln felt the same way. He said, 'The fact I don't want a Negress for my slave does not mean I want her for my wife.' And I have precedents in Nature for feeling the way I do."

"In Nature?"

"You've played into the Judge's hands now," said Harwood with a big smile.

"Yes, Nature is against miscegenation," continued Mills. "Do you see lions mating with tigers? Dogs and cats? Horses and cattle? Chickens and ducks? Nature keeps differing breeds from mating."

"I see," said Davis, unsmiling. "Any more examples?"

"Yes, Lee, plenty. In the air do we have eagles mating with falcons? Hummingbirds with sparrows? Or in the sea do we have dolphins with sharks, salmon with tuna? Do you want me to go on? I have plenty more. The whole gamut of living things."

"Well, Judge, you have made quite a case," said Davis, biding his time. "But there must be some exceptions."

"Lee, the only exception I know of is a horse mating with a donkey. The result is a mule. As you know a mule cannot beget any offspring, so Nature seems to take care of the miscegenation by stopping it right there."

"That's really too bad, Judge," interjected Harwood. "Because if you mated a mule with a cow you might get milk with a kick in it, and in these Prohibition days we could use it!"

"That's very funny, Oscar, but I'm serious," replied Mills, slowly. "Those are the facts, and it would seem that Nature is in agreement with my stance in the matter."

"The only trouble is," said Davis, as Mills gazed at him steadily, "we are dealing with humans, and animal-world rules don't seem to apply, although I must say again you have advanced an excellent argument for your thesis. But we are talking about a different color and not a different breed. A more logical and pertinent question would be, for example, would a white polar bear mate with a black grizzly bear. The answer, I think, is if you put them in the same cave they would. Color wouldn't matter to them. Isn't that a closer illustration?"

Mills was adamant. "No, it isn't Lee, because I believe they would fight and not mate." He paused a moment and then said, "I firmly believe in that case *that* would be Nature's way of preserving the breed."

"Judge, you're very persuasive. But tell me, getting back to blacks and whites, why was it that on Southern plantations the Negro had to use the back door to the mansions and was not permitted in any of the rooms except to clean them, but it was all right for white masters to welcome Negro slaves in the bedrooms? They didn't keep them out of the bedrooms, did they? On many a plantation the master's children and some of the slaves looked remarkably alike, which was quite a source of embarrassment to the lady of the plantation. Very embarrassing indeed!"

"Lee, I know some of that went on, but certainly not with the decent Southerners. Real Southern people of quality did not indulge in that."

"Are you sure of that, Judge? Would you include Thomas Jefferson in your Southern people of quality?"

"I certainly would, Lee. But knowing you, I guess I'm in for a surprise."

"Well, Judge, prepare yourself for a slight shock. Thomas Jefferson not only indulged in the bedroom, but he indulged quite regularly. He had four sons with a mulatto slave by the name of Sally Hemings. As the boys grew up they looked so much like him it caused laughter in the community, and Jefferson had to send them to the home of a friend in Pennsylvania. Do you want me to continue?"

"Lee, I assume from the way you are talking that you could name quite a few, but it really wouldn't prove anything. Let's forget that for the moment. Let us agree that whites and blacks are members of the human race. But still they're different. They have absolutely different cultures, different tastes, and different modes of living."

"I agree with that, Judge, but what's the point?"

"The point is we live differently, and there is quite a gulf between us. Take a very important difference—food. We are what we eat. Some people are vegetarians, and they are among the gentlest people in the world. Some people are cannibals, Lee, and I hardly think you would want to associate with them."

"Judge, I assume even cannibals are sociable, and I imagine they invite people to dinner. The only trouble is that the person invited to dinner may be the dinner."

"Lee, let's be serious. If anything indicates the backwardness of a people it's the food they eat. Food becomes a measure of our civilization. Why, in Africa some of the things they eat arc unbelievable, and white people couldn't possibly stomach it."

"Judge, you may be right that what we eat indicates how backward we are. It could be. I know of a large group of people so primitive that they love to eat the embryo of certain birds, and slices from the belly of certain animals. And they grind up grass seed, make it into a paste, and burn it over a fire. Then they smear it with a greasy mess they extract from the mammary fluid of animals."

"Lee, you're proving my point! There you have a barbaric people. What they eat proves it."

"I guess you're right, Judge, because what I have just described is the good old American breakfast of bacon and eggs and buttered toast."

Davis would always remember the expression on Judge Mills's face.

It was March 30, 1927, two years later, before the final determination of the Rhinelander case was made by the Court of Appeals. During this period Alice continued to receive temporary alimony. She made no effort to start an action for separation, since that would have resulted in the award of a similar amount and would have served no financial purpose. However, with the decision of the Court of Appeals, upholding Justice Morschauser and the Appellate Division, the temporary alimony stopped with the entry of judgment.

Leonard could voluntarily have continued to give Alice an allowance, but he apparently had no such intention. His feelings for her now bordered on hatred.

Alice no longer had a choice. On December 30, 1927, she

commenced an action for separation, charging cruel and inhuman treatment stemming from the open and public charges of fraud Leonard had made, which Alice claimed caused her "irreparable mental anguish and suffering."

The legal merry-go-round was moving again.

Alice didn't want Philip Rhinelander to think that he had been forgotten or was being neglected, and she started an alienation suit against him. When rumors circulated that a settlement was in the wind, somewhere in the neighborhood of two hundred to three hundred thousand dollars, Philip stated in private that that would happen "when the King of England is elected President of the United States."

Leonard, advised that the best defense was a strong offense, started an action for divorce in Nevada. He charged that "Mrs. Rhinelander took advantage of my youth and inexperience, dominated me, and induced me to forsake my family and friends so that they became estranged from me and I suffered humiliation and mental distress until my nervous condition became so acute . . . I separated from her."

Alice remained cool and unruffled when asked by the press to comment on this accusation. "It's absolutely ridiculous," she was quoted as saying. "It is just as if I was hit by an automobile driven by a reckless driver, and the driver sued me claiming my body dented his car."

It was now difficult to keep track of the cases, who was suing whom and where. All parties denied everything the others alleged, and reporters had little difficulty in getting the principals to talk, even Philip Rhinelander.

However, the stubborn elder Rhinelander had reached his limit—"This public display must be terminated!"—and finally decided to settle the escalating litigation so he could return to a life free from lawsuits and horrendous surveillance by the press.

A meeting was arranged for September 14, 1929, in Omaha, Nebraska, among Philip Rhinelander, Leonard, Alice, and their attorneys. (No one ever explained the curious choice of Omaha as a rendezvous point, although the question was asked of each of the principals by newsmen.)

There it was decided that the lawyers would get together and try to "resolve all differences." Translated, that meant, "How much money is to be paid to Alice?"

However, the stock-market crash of October 1929 forcibly altered Philip Rhinclanders' thinking. What he was willing to pay in September 1929, he was unwilling to pay in October.

Ten months later, on July 18, 1930, five years after the Rhinelander case began, it finally ended. Alice consented to Leonard's Nevada divorce, withdrew her suits against all parties, and received a cash settlement in the neighborhood of $215,000. It was golden balm to sooth the pain and humiliation she had suffered through five agonizing years.

For Alice the wheel had finally turned, and she made up for lost time. On a trip to London she was the center of attraction. Everywhere she went in England, it was the same. People who would have thought twice about hiring her as a housemaid five years previously were now jostling each other in their eagerness to snap her picture.

When she returned to the United States her ship was met by twenty reporters, clamoring for interviews. It was noted that the returning Governor of New Jersey was met by only five.

Alice Jones Rhinelander was almost as widely known as the motion-picture superstars of her day—not because of any accomplishment on her part on the stage or screen or in the world of music or art, but only because her color had rejected her for admission to the white world of Philip Rhinelander.

It was truly ironic. Thanks to Philip Rhinelander and his prejudices, Alice now had a measure of fame and wealth beyond her wildest dreams.

Barbara Hutton
and
Her Seven Husbands

It's been one unhappy ending after another for "the richest woman in the world" (a misnomer to begin with), the former "storybook princess," now sixty-three, whose real life has unfortunately turned out to be a grim fairy tale complete with seven unhappy trips to the altar.

Tens of thousands of young women worked long hours at low wages in Woolworth Five-&-Ten-Cent stores to provide Barbara Hutton millions of dollars to squander on her futile search for love.

Had she gone up to the top of her famous grandfather's Woolworth Building and scattered the millions to the four winds, the end result would have been the same. They were wasted millions. *Love* for Barbara Hutton was a will-o'-the-wisp that mockingly took the money and gave nothing in return.

Men have dominated and practically engulfed the life of broody Barbara. Personal fulfillment has totally eluded her. "The Poor Little Rich Girl's" fifty-million-dollar fortune hasn't bought her happiness, although it certainly has bought her the best legal brains in the business, an invaluable asset when a woman acquires and disposes of husbands as though they were jewels or real estate.

Barbara Hutton has captured and held the imagination of the public since she was a teenager. Until the 1960s, she en couraged publicity, despite her denials. Public-relations experts were often on the Hutton payroll to shape and maintain a suitable image for the lady who hated being described in print as "the melancholy millionairess" or other similar, but equally accurate, appellations.

Her marital affairs and private life have been covered by the media as though she were a movie star. Indeed, for all practical purposes, she *was* a movie star, without ever having had to go through the bother of making the movies. (It's not generally known that in the 1940s she actually considered entering motion pictures. Husband number three, Cary Grant, was firmly established in the Hollywood firmament but apparently chose not to encourage his wife's cinematic ambitions.)

Judging by her publicity, Barbara Hutton's driving ambition was to be the most *famous* woman in the world, and for a while she probably attained the goal. Much has been written about her over the years, and the facts of her colorful, complicated life have been distorted and mixed with large doses of fiction, fantasy, half-truths, and outright lies.

Many of Barbara's romantic escapades, particularly her involvement and marriage to Latin lover Porfirio Rubirosa, her affair with a Nazi prince prior to World War II, and her marriage to a German Baron once arrested by the Nazis for homosexuality, shocked her peers and excited tremendous gossip. But it can hardly be said that at any point did Barbara Hutton win people's sympathy or understanding, for which she seemed to yearn. It was hard to feel sorry for a woman who appeared to have both the physical and financial resources to wring the most from life but who in fact seemed to bungle things thoroughly. (At one point, in the 1930s, at the peak of the Depression, she threw an extravagant party that received wide publicity. She was bombarded by hate mail that caused her to remark, "I think I'm America's most hated girl.")

She certainly was one of America's most married girls. She was never attracted to obscure men, as far as potential mates were concerned. For husband material she sought out, and could afford, "the Big Ts"—titled men. Over the years she has paid more than seven million dollars in divorce settlements. The one Hutton husband who wasn't interested in taking Barbara's money was the commoner whose only title was Hollywood king. Cary Grant and Barbara have remained friends to the present day.

Barbara Hutton was born November 14, 1912, in New York City. Her grandfather was Frank Winfield Woolworth, who founded the Woolworth chain of five-and-dime stores throughout the country. Barbara's grandmother, Jennie, had serious mental problems. Frank and Jennie Woolworth had three daughters. Their youngest, Edna, was Barbara's mother.

Barbara's father was Franklyn Laws Hutton, who, at the time of his marriage, was a fiercely ambitious but not yet spectacularly successful broker on Wall Street. (His brother was E. F. Hutton.)

Edna and Franklyn Hutton hardly enjoyed a happy home life. (People would later wonder if Edna had inherited a fragment of her mother's illness.) When Barbara was born, the Huttons were living in downtown Manhattan at 2 East 8th Street, a fashionable section of Greenwich Village, just off Fifth Avenue. The home had been a gift to the newlyweds from Grandpa Woolworth. The Huttons also maintained a palatial apartment uptown, at the Plaza Hotel, at Fifth Avenue and 59th Street. The lavish hostelry would be the scene of the disaster whose repercussions would permanently reverberate throughout Barbara Hutton's life.

Franklyn Hutton, obsessed by the pursuit of his financial interests, ignored his wife and baby daughter. Edna Woolworth Hutton was deeply bothered that her husband spent so little time at home, and it was a dismal emotional existence for the woman. Tragedy was in store.

On May 2, 1917, when Barbara was four and a half, Edna Woolworth Hutton died—mysteriously. Discreet newspaper obituaries stated that the woman had died of an ear disease. However, speculation in private circles was that Edna had killed herself by jumping from the window of her Plaza apartment, and the whole nasty business had been effectively hushed up by the application of Woolworth cash to the proper palms.

After his wife's death Franklyn Hutton still took no interest in his daughter. Barbara grew to dislike her father intensely, and later claimed that on occasion he even struck her. Barbara also stated in later years that she considered her father, by dint of his gross negligence of her mother's state of mind, responsible for her death. Any chance that might have existed for Barbara and her father to enjoy something resembling a close family relationship died with Edna.

"I never knew my mother," lamented Barbara as an adult. "I hardly remember her. But I have missed her all my life. I think any girl's life takes on a different pattern when she is brought up without a mother."

However, Barbara was very fond of her grandfather, and he loved her. But Grandpa developed a nervous condition in his later years. Evenings spent at home would often consist of Grandpa and his nurse, Grandma and her "keeper"—and Barbara.

One of Grandpa's eccentricities was an incredible self-playing pipe organ, for which he bought a staggering number of perforated-paper rolls. They included hundreds of selections he had heard over the years, and loved. The Organ Room was paneled in carved oak and wired for weird effects. At the touch of a button the room would become completely dark. Then, depending on the music played, the lights would slowly come back on, changing colors. The effect was, to say the least, eerie, a real-life rendition of a scene from *Phantom of the Opera*. The organ could be heard in remote parts of the house and was even piped into the hollow bedposts of Grandpa's bed.

Another organ room "effect"—soft lights would illuminate paintings of composers on the walls. As the volume of the organ increased, lights over the portrait of the composer whose music was being played would intensify. "A guest might have the strange experience of listening to Die Walküre to an accompaniment of lightning flashes and sound effects reminiscent of roulades of thunder," remarked a visitor. "Then, out of the half-light there slowly materialized an ectoplasmic likeness of the composer."

The thoughts that must have passed through the mind of a sensitive child like Barbara, during these "concerts", can only be imagined. Perhaps she enjoyed such theatrics. There is no doubt she adored her grandfather, though Grandpa was particularly vocal on one subject: he loathed "titled foreigners on the hunt for rich American girls to marry."

He didn't live to see the parade of royalty through his beloved grand-daughter's life. He died when the child was seven. His will was unsigned, and his mentally incompetent wife, Jennie, inherited his fifty-million-dollar fortune.

Franklyn Hutton remained infatuated with the world of high finance and gave it all his attention. Barbara was sent to live with her Aunt Grace, her father's sister. Life for her there consisted of private schools, trips to Europe, and infrequent visits to and from daddy. Apparently the only fatherly advice Franklyn bothered to impart to his daughter was that people would always be attracted to her for one and only one reason—her money.

As a child, Barbara wasn't permitted many friends—youngsters were either considered not good enough for the young heiress or out to get something from her. Consequently, she was a loner almost from childhood.

But in her gilded cocoon she was coddled beyond belief by a staff of hand-picked servants. Even her food was tested to be sure it wasn't too hard to chew!

It's understandable that the young girl would begin to live in her own fantasies. Consequently, as she grew up, she was a difficult person to "get close to." Cary Grant would observe many years later that people inadvertently encouraged Barbara to remain distant because most people were intimidated by her great wealth and behaved like idiots in her presence.

And so her life was, and always would be, far from normal.

When Barbara turned twelve, Grandma Jennie died and Barbara inherited one-third of a fortune that had grown to seventy-five-million-dollars. Franklyn Hutton swiftly made investments for his daughter and increased her holdings substantially in a very short while.

Needless to say, another ten-million-dollars more or less would have no effect whatever on the young millionairess's lifestyle. But a bombshell shattered her private world in 1926 (Barbara was fourteen) when her father remarried. The new bride was Irene Curley Bodde, and Barbara initially disliked her. Over the years relations between Barbara and Irene would become cordial, almost warm, but after the first two years of his new marriage Franklyn Hutton arranged for

Barbara to move into her own apartment. This new dwelling would be no intimate four-or-five-room Central Park West hideaway. She was given two floors of a cooperative apartment her family owned at 1020 Fifth Avenue, which was remodeled at a cost of more than $250,000.

She was sent to Miss Hewitt's School in Manhattan, and during the year she met Cobina Wright, Sr., who was to become a close friend, one of the few Barbara would have. Mrs. Wright has recalled that while Barbara was "likeable," Franklyn Hutton was "a sick man, as every alcoholic is." Mrs. Wright pitied him. Barbara hated him.

Barbara began being "seen" in public, and soon she met a dashing socialite, Russian Prince Alexis Mdivani. Ten years older than Barbara and an established social climber, Mdivani was romantically involved with Astor heiress Louise Van Alen, a friend of Barbara's. But Barbara's fifty-million dollars were an irresistible attraction to the prince and he enthusiastically, indeed avidly, responded to the plump, plain girl's interest. She wrote him often, and he always responded. Did it matter that in the interim he and Miss Van Alen got married? Apparently not, not to him and not to Barbara. (Miss Van Alen never stated her feelings on the subject.)

"He was the only person who ever listened to me," Barbara recalled later. She poured out her heart to him. With Alex, her inferiority complex seemed to vanish. If to some he appeared a father figure, so what? "My father was too busy to be a real father," Barbara complained.

But Mdivani *was* married, so Barbara looked around and soon became engaged to a wealthy young playboy, Phil Plant. He had been married to screen star Constance Bennett. But Franklyn Hutton despised Plant and saw to it that Plant and Barbara didn't get married. However, Hutton couldn't stop his daughter from being noticed by the press, and noticed she was. She was great copy—"the Million-Dollar Baby who'll own the five-and-ten-cent stores"—and she loved seeing her name in print.

Barbara had lots of energy in those days and seemed to be having a good time. She was one of the world's most eligible "bachelorettes," and dated Tony Biddle, Winston Guest, Jimmy Blakely and Bobby La Branche. She adored traveling in Europe, and, in Biarritz, "ran into" Prince Mdivani at a party hosted by Parisian couturier Jean Patou. Barbara was "a young woman whose eyes were curiously expressionless and whose face was set in a mask of studied indifference"—until Mdivani's arrival. When she spotted the Prince, her face lit up and she became animated.

Mdivani was with his wife, Louise Van Alen. Completely ignoring her, he made a beeline for Barbara. Years later Barbara revealed that Mdivani was totally straightforward and rather unromantic regarding the possibility of divorcing Miss Van Alen and marrying Barbara.

"You wouldn't want to marry me, Barbara. My price is too high," he told her.

What was his price?

"Two million dollars, cash."

"All right."

It was as simple as that.

They were married on June 22, 1933, five months before Barbara's twenty-first birthday. It was the peak of the Depression, and Woolworth executives were furious about the mocking publicity flooding the newspapers before and after the dazzling wedding, which took place at the Russian Cathedral in Paris. Mdivani's wedding present to Barbara was a magnificent jade necklace, for which she subsequently paid.

Barbara was hardly a public-relations asset to the popular chain of five-and-tens whose employees and customers could only resent and despise Barbara's empress-like lifestyle when people were financially desperate. The average five-and-ten saleswoman was earning around ten dollars a week! Barbara's annual income was about nine hundred thousand dollars, and her fortune was growing at the rate of more than two million dollars a year.

But Barbara considered herself answerable only to herself. "I wanted a companion," she explained. And Mdivani was the man she wanted. His social credentials were far from flawless. His father, Zakhari Mdivani, had been a general of infantry in the Czar's army, not a glamorous figure at court. American title hunters, however, happily overlooked the fact that the title "Prince" was a nominal one in old Russia. The Mdivanis had fled their country after the Bolshevik revolution. When they arrived in Paris, Mama Mdivani, of Polish ancestry, registered herself at a police station as Princess Mdivani. By so doing she assured a life of luxury for her ambitious sons.

Jean Patou said of the Mdivanis: "They come from Georgia, and anyone who owned three sheep in that part of Russia before the war automatically was a nobleman." One pillar of society described Alexis Mdivani as "a scion of a distinguished line of sheepherders." (There was also a Mdivani sister, who, in the late 1920s, made headlines when she broke up the marriage of famed Spanish artist José Maria Sert.)

Alexis and his brothers, Prince David and Prince Serge, were seasoned professionals in the marriage game. They were prime examples of lower-case royalty appealing to nouveau-riche society. David had been married to silent-movie queen Mae Murray when she was at the height of her career. He was instrumental in dissipating her fortune. Serge had been married to Pola Negri. But to many observers the "marrying Mdivanis," as they were known, were a joke—men whose charm and ability to flatter had carried them far.

If Prince Mdivani's price had been high, Barbara Hutton

got what she wanted from him—a title. As a child she liked to be called "Princess Barbara," and now it was official. Barbara was honest when confronted with facts about Mdivani's questionable "princehood." "People shouldn't cast aspersions on a title," she said. "That's just gossip. It's going to be fun to be a Princess and Alexis has a right to be proud."

When she married Mdivani he immediately received from Barbara a $50,000 annual income. But he didn't respond to Barbara's generosity in a kindly manner. He often criticized her appearance. "Why can't you be sleek like a European?" was a sample comment. "You're fat as a pig" was another. She embarked on a grueling diet and lost fifty pounds. She was not unaware of the hazards of a "don't eat" regimen. "Dangerous? Well, perhaps. But I want to keep a figure like Mahatma Ghandi. It's easy. Every so often I go on a strict coffee diet. I drink only one cup of coffee three times a day and eat nothing for three weeks."

This was the beginning of an unending, dangerous cycle of starvation diets that would ruin her health, all in the interest of keeping her weight down to a chic and flattering one hundred pounds.

On November 14, 1933, she turned twenty-one and formally inherited her fifty-million-dollar fortune. Her fantastic twenty-six-room apartment on Fifth Avenue was the scene of a fabulous party at which she could officially celebrate her new status as a free agent.

Her confidant now, and he would be until his death, was her cousin Jimmy Donahue. Barbara and Jimmy had a common bond—her mother and his father had both taken their own lives. Donahue could make Barbara laugh, and his wild sense of humor provided what Barbara even then considered the only light in her life.

She needed all the laughs Donahue could supply in order

to weather the vehement disapproval of her lifestyle constantly voiced in the press. Typical was columnist Ed Sullivan's blast via an "open letter" in the Daily News: "The unreality of your existence must be boring, Princess. You have a husband who has little or no relation to everyday life . . . Here we are, face to face with stark realities, stark distress, and your Prince is spending American dollars on toys that gratify his own vanity . . ."

Obviously Sullivan then had to gratify *his* own vanity by showing readers that his contacts with underworld figures were as impressive as those of number one columnist Walter Winchell. Quoting opinions voiced by gangsters, Sullivan wrote a threatening putdown of Prince Mdivani: "I have heard underworld chieftans speak about him [Mdivani] and his apparently callous disregard for human suffering, and I would not want them to speak that way about me. I would dislike to turn him loose among the waterfront of New York . . . they might do some dreadful things to him and make it impossible for him to play polo again."

Barbara's advisors didn't ignore the column, nor did they ignore Sullivan's suggestion that Barbara establish "an annual Princess Barbara Christmas dinner by contributing 1000 Christmas baskets to the poor. The whole thing wouldn't amount to $5000, and out of it you'd get $50,000 worth of honest-to-God happiness."

It was practically blackmail, but Barbara donated the $5000. Sullivan subsequently wrote, "Princess Barbara is the Tops," and called her a "swell person—just swell!"

Princess Mdivani, however, was growing bored with her expensive Prince. They took a whirlwind tour of Europe and the Orient in early 1934, a sort of second honeymoon. Barbara adored Chinese culture—"there's no catty hostility in China" —and spent tens of thousands of dollars acquiring oriental art. Jimmy Donahue went along on this trip. But Barbara couldn't fool herself about her collapsing marriage, and she began what would become a pattern in her life. Whenever a personal crisis arose, she would take to her bed—alone.

By the end of 1934 Barbara, still married to Mdivani, had met the man who would be her next husband. A later husband described Barbara's falling in love as follows: "She is absolutely crazy when love strikes her. Yes, crazy! When the hormones start to move around in her body, it affects her. She starts the poems and this and that."

Barbara was an avid poetry writer. It was a talent for which she received little praise and encouragement. A limited edition of her poems had been published privately by Faber and Faber in London. The volume was entitled *The Enchanted*. "Now I suppose people who read them will say, 'Why doesn't the young lady take up gardening instead?'" said Barbara. "The truth is, I shall never attempt to have my poetry printed publicly for two very good reasons. First, the poems are not good enough. And second, because people would not buy them for the poetry but because they want to see just what sort of nonsense I had written. But I shall continue to write because I like to."

And of course she also liked handsome men and would continue to pursue them. The prince's successor in Barbara's affections was the six-foot Prussian-born nobleman, Count Court Haugwitz-Reventlow, described by Barbara as "the handsomest person I ever saw." Franklyn Hutton, dubious about Count Reventlow's background, had him investigated. But the aristocrat's credentials were impeccable, and Barbara had made up her mind to marry him. There was a seventeen-year age difference—Barbara was twenty-two, and Reventlow was thirty-nine. But that hardly mattered to the prospective bride.

Barbara journeyed to Reno, the prelude to her divorce from Mdivani. (High Society savant Elsa Maxwell later observed: "I can't help wondering whether Barbara's first marriage set the pattern for subsequent failures by accentuating as it did her deep-seated inferiority complex.")

On May 13, 1935, Barbara's divorce action was tried in Reno's Washoe County Courthouse. Her attorney was Millard Thomkins, Jr., and the procedure took eleven minutes. Barbara testified she was "a polo widow" and had been "cruelly mistreated." There was no community property, no children. Total attourneys' fees and court costs for Barbara amounted to a hundred thousand dollars, and Mdivani's settlement, in cash and real estate, was close to three million dollars. The prince died in an auto accident a couple of years later and publicly Barbara expressed shock and sorrow. But in private her reaction wasn't hypocritical: "Thank heaven. Now I won't run into him every time we're at the same hotel!"

Life with Barbara Hutton was obviously not all solid gold. If her father was obsessed with business, she was equally obsessed with her appearance. She was in tears when she gained even a few ounces and literally starved herself to avoid putting on any weight. Count Reventlow tried to convince her that a little weight looked attractive, but she would have none of it. Concerned for her health, he took her to a famed dietary clinic in Germany, where the doctors found that Barbara maintained one ironclad rule: you won't gain weight if you don't eat.

Barbara was voicing a new complaint—she could no longer stand being followed everywhere by reporters. There had been a flood of unfavorable publicity in America when she married Reventlow. Even religious figures commented on it. "The marital troubles of Barbara Hutton," said Rabbi Abraham L. Feinberg in a sermon at Mount Neboh Temple, "prove that real happiness cannot be bought. Barbara Hutton should forget counts who spend her money and remember counter girls who earn it."

A priest, the Reverend Eugene J. MacDonald, a professor at Cathedral College, stated: "It's unjust that girls in the five-and-ten stores are getting 12 to 15 dollars a week when the heiress to the Woolworth fortune is living in Europe spending her money lavishly in foreign countries and married to a foreigner."

It is understandable that Barbara wanted "no more publicity." Her husband believed she meant it. He spoke with important newspaper editors, imploring them to please let up on covering the life of Barbara Hutton Reventlow. One expressed sympathy and said he'd see what he could do. A few weeks later Barbara called his newspaper and complained that she was being ignored. "Am I dead?" she asked. Publicity was apparently a necessity to her, and only when she wasn't receiving any would she really grumble.

Barbara became pregnant. According to her husband, she was "distraught and perplexed" at this development. She would have no choice but to gain weight now! Irritable, she went to London to await the birth of her child. She insisted on a cesarean delivery, despite protestations by her obstetrician, Doctor Cedric Lane-Roberts.

He was right, and there were serious complications. Barbara's condition worsened, and she went into a coma. The physician to King Edward, Lord Horder, was called in. Members of the Hutton family and Jimmy Donahue flew to London as Barbara went through a desperate medical crisis. A second operation was necessary. Barbara came through it, and newspapers subsequently reported that blood from Red Cross donors and not the blood of her wealthy friends or relatives, had saved Barbara's life.

Her child was a healthy, beautiful boy. She named him Lance. With the birth of the baby the Reventlow residence in London was guarded round the clock by a squadron of private detectives, a precaution against kidnapping. (The Lindbergh baby had been kidnapped a few years previously, with traumatic effect on wealthy parents in both the United States and Europe. Barbara had even expressed fear of being kidnapped herself.)

Baby Lance's nursery consisted of a three-room suite, with two bathrooms. The tinted walls featured life-sized paintings of children.

Barbara, having decided to make England more or less a permanent home, made plans to build a fantastic residence for herself. Winfield House was subsequently constructed. The original estimate for the house was three million dollars, but with changes and alterations, it wound up at a staggering cost of more than five million.

Such extravagance again guaranteed terrible public-relations problems for Barbara back in the United States. She was in urgent need of good advice regarding her relations with the press, and it was suggested she agree to an interview with noted Hearst writer Adela Rogers St. Johns. Barbara said yes, and the resulting article brought her the best publicity she had ever had. "Babs hasn't had an awful lot of happiness," wrote Adela. "Along the road she has found that there are an awful lot of things you can't buy—things that the most ordinary kid in the world possesses without trouble." Barbara told Adela, "I am only one generation removed from the women of my family who washed their own dishes and made their own clothes. I have a hunch if I had to go back to the dishpan, I could do it." Why had she moved to England?

"I left America because they said and wrote such unkind things about me. I couldn't stand people disliking me so much and always thinking the worst of me, so I came away. That is why I am living in England, where they don't pay any attention to me."

In a statement that was totally laughable to those who knew Barbara Hutton intimately, Barbara claimed: "I'm not under any illusions about myself. I don't give a hoot for social position. We haven't any, really—how could we have? If we didn't have all this money, we couldn't be in the Social Register."

Adela later said, "I felt damn sorry for her, and I hoped she was going to make it." She pointed out that certain girls, and Barbara was one of them, were meant to be "fat, husky, healthy girls." Adela felt Barbara got into trouble when she "did the coffee diet and ruined her health forever." And furthermore there were all those people who had made poor Barbara believe she wasn't pretty. "The story of Barbara is so sad. It's heartbreaking."

Equally heartbreaking were Count Reventlow's attempts to participate positively in certain areas of Barbara's life. She was an avid collector of priceless jewels, and Reventlow made the mistake of trying to save her money in this pursuit. She had decided she wanted to own the famous Leeds-McCormick emeralds. They had belonged to opera singer Ganna Walska and were supposedly valued at $1.2 million. (Originally owned by Napoleon III, he had given the eight flawless emeralds to his mistress, the Contessa di Castiglione.) Cartier offered them to Barbara for nine hundred thousand dollars, and she didn't blink an eye. But Reventlow felt the price was outrageous and consulted an appraiser, who explained there were only a few families who could afford such a purchase and their assets were subject to sudden change. "I believe if you had to sell overnight, the most you could get would be around $250,000."

Reventlow entered the bargaining and offered Cartier three hundred thousand dollars. The jewelers said no. Soon, however, they capitulated and agreed to a price slightly over Reventlow's bid. Ecstatic, Reventlow wrote out a check and asked Barbara to sign it. She told him she didn't want the emeralds anymore. The whim had passed.

Reventlow, however, was in an embarrassing position. He had bargained in good faith with Cartier, and his reputation was on the line. He explained to Barbara that if she didn't sign the check he would have to make out his own, although the amount would leave him penniless.

Barbara signed the check, but the emeralds had come into her possession after she no longer wanted them, and she almost never wore them.

However, she could well afford the jewels. Wrote Associated Press, "The Bureau of Internal Revenue disclosed today that Barbara Hutton, the Woolworth heiress, was worth more than $45 million in 1933, and that $32 million of this sum was invested in tax-exempt securities of the United States government."

No expense was spared in making her London palace, Winfield House, second in opulence only to Buckingham Palace. The treasures it contained included a rug in the drawing room that Barbara adored. It had belonged to Louis XIV, and she bought it for sixty-five thousand dollars. But it made Count Reventlow nervous to walk on it. Barbara, however, liked the rug, and it remained in the house.

While Barbara lived in splendor in Europe, trouble was brewing for her at home. On March 17, 1937, Woolworth employees went on strike for a minimum wage of twenty dollars a week. They sent Barbara a cablegram: HUNGER

STRIKERS IN NEW YORK ASK YOUR INTERVENTION FOR A LIVING WAGE, and on the streets of New York they chanted a parody of a famous song:

> *Barbara Hutton's got the dough, parlay voo;*
> *We know where she got it, too, parlay voo;*
> *We share at Woolworth's five-and-dime,*
> *The pay we get is sure a crime,*
> *Hinky dinky, parlay voo.*

Barbara and her husband were in Cairo when she received the cablegram. She was very upset—she had nothing to do with the management of Woolworth stores—and she took to bed immediately. Her "no comment" was not met with a happy reaction by the strikers. "She certainly has a lot to say about really *important* matters, like the King of England's affair with Mrs. Wallis Simpson," snarled some editorials. Barbara's comment about that had been, "Please remember, *every* woman has the right to a life of her own."

Barbara was on the verge of a decision that would have quite a damaging effect on her future public relations. She was paying a fortune in American income taxes, although she was not living in the United States, and her advisors presented her with a plan.

Step one was for her to meet with James W. Gerard, a career diplomat, former United States ambassador to Germany and a close friend of President Roosevelt. The purpose of the meeting became obvious when Gerard subsequently told the press that Barbara Hutton was proud to be an American and should be given a medal for not having relinquished her citizenship "although she could have done so and saved large sums of money in income taxes." He said that Barbara wanted to come back to the United States, "if you fellows will give her a chance."

Step two in the Hutton plan, to the dismay and embarrassment of James Gerard, since he obviously hadn't known he had been step one, was for Barbara to give up her American citizenship. The ostensible reason for this was that she was spending money on such a grand scale that in time she could go broke unless some dramatic measures were adopted at once. Her income at this time was close to two million dollars a year, before taxes. But she had spent more than four million on jewelry alone during the first year of her marriage to Reventlow.

The planned solution was to make a special arrangement with the Treasury that would cut down Barbara's taxes in England and literally eliminate her American income taxes. But she would have to give up her citizenship to accomplish this, and it would have to be done in the United States.

Barbara was fearful, and with good reason, that the American press would crucify her when they learned of her intentions. (Woolworth stores never advertised, and Barbara often bemoaned this fact, since her corporation couldn't bring pressure to bear on newspapers by threatening to withdraw advertising revenue.)

At this point Graham D. Mattison, a brilliant young attourney who worked for Barbara's Wall Street law firm, White and Case, came into her life. Only thirty-two years old, Mattison was to be the guiding legal light in Barbara's life. It was he who devised the strategy whereby Barbara could renounce her American citizenship without publicity while she was in the United States: arrive in New York on the morning of the day the papers were to be signed, go straight to the courthouse, appear before the judge and leave for Europe that evening.

The plan was successful, and she was safely out of the country when the storm broke. Woolworth employees went wild. Pickets carried signs: WHILE WE'RE ON STRIKE FOR HIGHER PAY, BABS TAKES HER MILLIONS AND RUNS AWAY!

Newspaper editorial writers had a field day. "No one here will miss Barbara Hutton," they wrote, "but the government will miss the tax revenues."

Barbara Hutton has never moved to get her citizenship back.

In the spring of 1938 Count Reventlow knew that his marriage was on very shaky ground. He recognized the early warnings. On a trip to India Barbara became interested in Prince Muassam Jah of Hyderabad, and soon Reventlow discovered that the prince and Barbara were writing intimate letters to each other. He exploded, and the Indian prince was the reason for many of their subsequent quarrels.

Then, later in the year, in London, Barbara became infatuated with twenty-six-year-old Prince Frederick of Prussia, a Nazi. His grandfather had been Kaiser Wilhelm II, and Barbara went so far as to remark to her husband, "Just think, Court. I could marry the man who might someday be the Emperor of Germany." This was only a short while before Germany started World War II! Apparently Barbara's life was totally insulated from certain harsh facts of what was happening in the world—or she simply did not care.

Barbara's attorney, William Mitchell, soon called on Count Reventlow to inform him that Countess Barbara wanted a divorce. Reventlow wasn't agreeable. A messy situation was in the works, culminating in a series of spectacular legal maneuvers attempting to embarrass Count Reventlow. At one point, Reventlow was actually arrested and held in two thousand pounds' bail for allegedly threatening his wife with bodily harm and threatening to shoot "an unnamed gentleman." But the Danish count was literally above reproach and emerged unscathed. And there was one tie that would bind Reventlow and Barbara together throughout their lives—their son.

Although Barbara had had a neglected childhood, she now seemed to bestow the same fate upon her son. He was usually in the care of his nurse. Lance would have a mother who was with him only when it suited her, and his father was not welcomed by her friends.

In spite of all efforts on Reventlow's part the marriage to Barbara was soon over. The Count was being referred to in newspapers as "The Melancholy Dane." On July 28, 1938, they signed separation papers and an agreement to obtain a divorce. Barbara would keep Lance nine months of the year. Reventlow would have approval of the boy's tutors, governesses, and so on, and jurisdiction over his education. While it was reported the count had received a settlement of $1 million prior to the marriage and $500,000 after, the truth is that no money settlement was involved. Reventlow was, however, made the trustee of a $1.5 million fund for Lance.

Reventlow remarked: "If the word *money* had not been an open sesame in Barbara's life she would be a much happier person today." But, of course, it's likely that their paths would never have crossed if Barbara hadn't been who she was. Reventlow attempted to reconcile with Barbara, but it was hopeless.

"Poor Court," she remarked. "I feel sorry for him, in a way. He's still living in the time of the Czars." Barbara said that he'd wince when she'd speak to the servants or do anything that didn't befit a royal personage. Barbara finally became exasperated and felt compelled to tell her husband, "Who cares? Who cares about the Count von Haughwitz-Reventlow. today? The world has come a long way from that sort of thing."

This seems an unlikely story, however. Barbara's favorite motion picture that year, one she urged Reventlow to see, reflected Barbara's true lifestyle and her state of mind: *Marie Antoinette.* MGM's lavish vehicle presented Norma Shearer as the ill-fated French queen. It was a romanticized, glamorous portrait of "poor Antoinette," who was pictured in a sympathetic, somewhat unrealistic light.

According to the film, Marie Antoinette's life was one long search for the right man. She was simply a woman in search of love, manipulated by those around her and misunderstood by an entire nation. Tyrone Power played a count in the film, the man with whom Antoinette falls hopelessly in love. Barbara said she thought the Power character reminded her of Reventlow.

Reventlow never saw the film, although he remarked, "Maybe I should have."

Late in 1939, as war clouds darkened over Europe, Barbara returned to New York. She would have no choice now but to attempt to reinstate herself in the good graces of the American public, and this wouldn't be easy. Alarming proof of people's resentment occurred when, in front of a theatre in New York, Barbara was insulted by a crowd calling her "a rich bitch."

Steve Hannagan (soon to be known in Hollywood circles as the man "Oomph Girl" Ann Sheridan was madly in love with) was hired to repair the damage Barbara had done to her image over the past few years.

Hannagan's program to restore the heiress to the good graces of the press would prove shrewd and successful. His ploy—have her "sell humility." Bargara gave selected interviews and posed for pictures knitting sweaters and socks for the Red Cross. She also posed with Lance at the New York World's Fair, looking the epitome of young American motherhood.

But Barbara was Barbara, and no one could change that. One evening, dining at the chic nightclub El Morocco with a titled friend, she was heard to say, "Isn't this dreadful, darling? You and I are the only royalty present!"

However, Barbara could be charming and captivating, "just folks," when she wanted to, and on a one-to-one basis, reporters found themselves liking her. Hannagan instructed her never to wear fabulous jewels in public: "People would resent such things."

Barbara's divorce would become final in the spring of 1941, and she had found a new playmate, a handsome young athlete named Robert Sweeney. As far as Sweeney was concerned, marriage was on the agenda. Society columnists, including "Cholly" Knickerbocker, agreed. Certainly marrying an American would be great for Barbara's new image. Her friend Adela Rogers St. Johns wrote, "I don't think we should forget that in Barbara's mind, at least, she gave up America because it first gave her up."

But the truth was that Barbara would always prefer Europe, Europeans, and the European way of life. The war had *forced* her back to the United States. The graciousness and gentility of the Old World manner were her cup of tea; the fast pace of American life was distasteful to her.

A *San Francisco Chronicle* columnist was tipped off to an amusing occurrence involving Barbara at this time. She was staying at the Hotel Mark Hopkins and found herself short of change. She sent one of the bellboys to the bank to change a large bill. The bill was in an envelope, and when the bellboy presented it to the teller, there was a gasp: Barbara had given the boy a ten-thousand-dollar bill to change.

This resulted in a flurry of bad publicity, the tone being resentful, pointing out that when most people did not earn that much money in two years, here was someone using it for small change. But Barbara survived the scoldings in print, and Hannagan's office counteracted the barrage by informing the press that Barbara gave away huge sums to charity, and was it fair to ignore that?

Barbara was candid with one reporter who asked her, "How many people do you suppose would be polite to me if my column were suddenly out of print?" Barbara replied, "I can top that one. How many people do you think would be nice to me if I lost all my money tomorrow?"

Barbara now was actually in a better state of mind than she'd been in for years. She was entering what could be described as her Hollywood Phase. She had been introduced to the man who would be her third husband—and it wasn't Bob Sweeney. Born Archibald Alexander Leach, the new man was a "commoner" but also a "King": Cary Grant, Hollywood's top heartthrob.

Barbara hadn't bothered to tell an astonished Bob Sweeney that he was out of the running; she didn't like scenes and avoided the inevitable until the last possible moment. Such had been her strategy with Prince Mdivani and Count Revent-low, both of whom learned of their successors after the fact.

Cary Grant and Barbara had been introduced by leading Hollywood social figure Countess Dorothy di Frasso. (In the late 1940s, Countess di Frasso's great love was the decidedly non—*Social Register* mobster Bugsy Siegel.)

Grant and Barbara telephoned each other frequently. But neither Cary nor "Babs," as the press constantly called her, were in any hurry. In fact, Barbara's true affections might indeed have lain elsewhere, as events would soon prove. The usual denials—"We're just good friends"—constantly made the rounds of gossip columns.

In the midst of her publicized romance with Cary Grant, Barbara received word that her father was seriously ill in Charleston. She had no feelings for the man and had no intention of flying to him. (As she would later say: "All the unhappiness in my life has been caused by men, starting with my father.") But friends finally convinced her it was bad for her image—she had to go. So she did. But Franklyn Hutton died without regaining consciousness.

Hutton willed his daughter no property or cash—"I realize that my beloved daughter Barbara is possessed in her own right of worldly goods ample for her future comfort"—but he did will her "a loving father's blessing for her future happiness."

Although Barbara's father bequeathed no money, she saw no reason not to get back money she had loaned him, and she sued his estate for repayment of $530,000, plus 5 percent interest. She won the suit. According to Barbara's stepmother Irene, the suit meant nothing—it was only "an arrangement between Barbara and her father." That statement lifted a few eyebrows.

Cary Grant courted Barbara at her incredible estate on Benedict Canyon Road in Beverly Hills. Nobles of various nationalities, "exiled" by the war, seemed to find their way to Barbara's. Many years later, referring to Barbara's preference for titled personages as social companions, Grant remarked, "If one more phony Earl had come in, I'd have suffocated."

Grant's close friends Rosalind Russell, her fiancé, Frederick Brisson (Grant had introduced them), David Niven, and

James Stewart frequently visited and kept things from getting too "heavy."

By March 1941, Barbara's divorce from Reventlow became final, and everyone expected her to marry Cary Grant immediately. She didn't. In later years Adela Rogers St. Johns wrote, "I think she kept him waiting two years, telling herself how lucky she was, that she ought to love him but knew in her heart she didn't."

Mrs. St. Johns knew her facts, because during Barbara's courtship with Cary there was a startling revelation—she had been regularly telephoning a German baron, and this was after World War II had started!

Columnist Drew Pearson broke the sensational story: "The former Princess Mdivani, apparently deeply in love with this German sportsman, and not interested in his Nazi views, has made a practice of taking a private plane from Hollywood to Mexico, where she placed transatlantic phone calls to the Baron." One of the Baron's cousins apparently was the intermediary and arranged for the calls in neutral Switzerland.

"Barbara did not suspect that every word she said to the Baron was taken down by censors," wrote Pearson. "But not long ago she either cooled off on the Baron or learned that he worked for the German government. For she sent him a cable instructing him not to communicate with her anymore."

The story was an A bomb as far as public opinion was concerned. And curiosity was intense regarding "who the hell this Nazi Baron was" who made "the Hutton-tot's pulse race even when she was about to marry one of Hollywood's all-time sex symbols." He was the Baron Gottfried Von Cramm, tennis buff and playboy, well-known to members of Barbara's set. (He had designed the tennis courts for Barbara's fabulous Winfield House.)

Cary Grant admitted he knew Barbara had been phoning

Von Cramm. "I didn't question it. The Baron was a very dear and old friend. And he was not a Nazi."

A final revelation: When Barbara was phoning Von Cramm from Mexico, the Baron had recently been released from a Nazi prison after serving a year for homosexuality. Von Cramm's cronies later stated that the Nazis were punishing the Baron for speaking against Hitler, and various highborn Europeans had pleaded for his release.

Incredibly, Barbara was not finished with Von Cramm, not by a long shot. But for the duration of the war, she had no choice. The furor died down and on July 10, 1942, Barbara Hutton Mdivani Reventlow, thirty, and Cary Grant, thirty-eight, were married at Lake Arrowhead by the Reverend H. Paul Romeis, of the English Lutheran Church in San Bernadino. It was Grant's second marriage.

The six-minute ceremony, at the home of Frank Vincent, was ultra-private, and Grant saw to it that it *didn't* leak to the press until after the wedding. (Could Barbara have been happy about that?)

In Cary Grant Barbara had selected a man who actually cherished his privacy and scoffed at movie star–type publicity. Grant was incredibly adept at maintaining his privacy and saw to it that the press was kept out of Barbara's life too. He even convinced her not to employ Steve Hannagan any longer, a move she would later regret.

Life at the Grants hardly reflected wartime austerity. The staff included Lance's nurse, Barbara's personal maid, Grant's secretary, valet, chauffeur-masseur and eleven servants. Grant was not without a sense of humor. "The servants had so many shifts to feed at mealtime that Barbara and I were lucky to get a sandwich." On Sunday, servants' day off, Barbara and

Cary were alone and she prepared dinner, usually chicken à la king.

Cary was the only Hutton husband who could afford to buy Barbara gifts with his own money. He was the only one of Barbara's husbands who had a paying profession, a steady job. Consequently she had more time on her hands than ever before. She began writing poetry again and years later Grant confessed, "Unfortunately, and to my shame, I had little knowledge of poetry, and I didn't encourage her. She had a need for expression, but I had little patience for it. I regret I gave her no encouragement, and I think few people have. That is as much responsible for her unhappiness as anything."

Grant and Barbara actually had little in common. Their friends and ideas were different. Barbara thought perhaps she should try the acting profession. It was suggested that she would be the perfect leading lady for her husband in his upcoming picture for RKO, *Mr. Lucky*, the story of a gambler who becomes enamored of "an heiress-type lady."

Grant gave her no encouragement here either. He was against the idea. "I saw no reason for her doing it." Those on the scene say he outright opposed her doing it, and Laraine Day got the role.

Perhaps this would have been Barbara's outlet for expression, but she didn't pursue it.

Barbara confided to Hedda Hopper and her millions of readers: "Cary and I would love to have a baby. We talk about it all the time." This, too, was not in the cards. Barbara had had an ovary removed after her son's birth in London, and specialists contend that this was probably the reason she never conceived again.

There were long periods when Barbara "wasn't feeling well" and had to remain in bed. Cary's opinion of Barbara's various "ailments," operations, and consultations with many doctors:

"Barbara was cut to ribbons long before I knew her." In Grant's view, Barbara's bankroll was reason enough for surgeons to want to operate immediately. "After all," said Grant, "when you become a surgeon you justify all your behavior for that fee. They're not doing it for Barbara. They're doing it for them. Those scars were all from that bankroll."

Grant was constantly aware that Barbara was never treated normally by anyone. People were tongue tied and said ridiculous and stupid things because they were so awed by how much money she had. Cary understood how her wealth affected people, and he hated it.

In the interests of making the marriage work, Grant insisted that two of Barbara's servants, women who were her intimate confidantes and who were described by both former and later husbands as troublemakers, not live on the premises after regular working hours. They complied.

But his efforts to make the marriage work didn't bear fruit. Some of Barbara's society-columnist friends were enraged that Barbara, a colorful source of news, had been cut off from them by Grant's "no publicity" attitude. Igor Cassini referred to Grant in print as a former hot dog vendor at Coney Island. Grant fumed that he had never sold a hot dog in his life. "If I had, I'd have a chain of hot dog stands by now."

Despite Grant's attempts to avoid publicity, he and his wife were sitting ducks. He was snidely referred to by some columnists as "Cash and Cary," and others wrote that the movie idol was becoming bored with his marriage and had taken to playing practical jokes that embarrassed Barbara in front of her "snooty" friends.

Others implied that it was Barbara who was bored. But there was truth to the rumors that the marriage was in trouble.

Barbara was having other personal problems that made

news. Count Reventlow was seething because he feared Barbara was turning their son against him. He had proof of this, inadvertently supplied by comments the boy had made.

Then embarrassing publicity of a different sort emerged when it was revealed that Barbara and Cary had given letters of recommendation to a handsome young man, complete with title, who turned out to be a foreign agent being trailed by the FBI. The Grants said they had been hoodwinked.

It was again the end of the marital trail for Barbara. She and Grant were about to separate when Barbara was hit by a lawsuit from Reventlow, regarding Lance. Babs immediately added Hollywood's number-one troubleshooter, lawyer Jerry Geisler, to her entourage of attorneys. (Geisler clients included Charles Chaplin, Errol Flynn, and later Lana Turner and Marilyn Monroe.)

In the midst of all this, Barbara was the "star" of a "warm" human interest story on her own home territory. Her devoted personal maid and her chauffeur had fallen in love. They were married, and Barbara personally handled all details, including a reception in her home. Later, the ex-chauffeur, Harry Leach (no relation to Cary Grant), would be quoted as saying, "Miss Hutton is the most marvelous girl in the world. She always lives ritzy because she's got to, but she isn't ritzy. She's got a sense of humor about everything." When the Leaches encountered financial difficulties years later, Barbara came to their rescue.

When the Reventlow debacle died down, Grant and Barbara separated.

It came to light that before officially divorcing Grant, Barbara was dating another handsome actor, Philip Reed. In later years Reed observed: "Cary hated my guts and he thought I was breaking up his marriage, but it was already finished. Cary was very difficult about it at first. He resented me very much at the time and said some very nasty things about me. Barbara came back from him in tears one day because he was loud in his opinion concerning me, none of which she believed."

Reed also stated, "I am probably the only one who never got anything from her because I just wouldn't accept it. She wanted to buy a house for me when I got out of the Navy, but I would have no part of it. We were in love. I thought we would marry, and so did she. But I didn't want to go down in history as being one of many who was kept by her."

According to Reed, "If the war hadn't ended and Von Cramm came back into the picture, we would have been married. And if we had, it would have ended like everything else. She just doesn't have the capacity to sustain anything."

In August 1945, six weeks after their third wedding anniversary, Barbara Hutton divorced Cary Grant.

Grant was not present at the hearing.

Appearing before Superior Court Judge Thurmond Clarke, Jerry Geisler questioned Barbara.

"Now, you allege that since the marriage he has caused you great mental cruelty. Kindly explain that to the court."

"Well," said Barbara, "Mr. Grant and myself did not have the same friends. Mr. Grant didn't like my friends and I didn't like his friends.

"On more than one occasion, when I gave dinner parties he would not come downstairs but would have dinner in bed. When he did come down, he just didn't seem amused."

"How did this affect you?" Judge Clarke asked.

"It made me rather nervous."

"Did you require services of a doctor?"

"Yes I did."

Germaine Tocquet, one of Barbara's servants whom Grant had excluded from their home after working hours, corroborated Mrs. Grant's testimony. "Mr. Grant did not like her friends. On many occasions he excused himself. This made her very embarrassed."

"How else did it affect her?" queried Mr. Geisler.

"It made her nervous."

"That's enough, decree granted," concluded Judge Clarke.

In later years Cary Grant observed, "I'm not at all sure that either of us really wanted to marry the other by the time we got around to it. I thought too much about my career and not enough about her. I suppose I was emotionally immature. I persisted in my stupidities."

They had, of course, had some good times together. "Barbara had a marvelous word for anything that lacks taste," recalled Grant. " 'My God, isn't that *ig*,' she'd say. Once we visited a pink Italian villa in Burlingame, California. The house was done in delightful taste, except for one thing— there was a great apricot-colored bar stretching across one whole end of the living room. The owner was exceptionally proud of it, and she finally said, 'Don't you just love the bar?' There was a pause, and then I said, 'Yes, it's so wonderfully *ig*.' Well, I tell you, Barbara got hysterical with laughter. She staggered around the room shrieking and she was still doubled up when we got to the car."

Thanks to Barbara, Grant had acquired an appreciation of fine paintings. After their divorce, they remained on such friendly terms that Barbara gave Cary's next wife, actress Betsy Drake, twenty fabulous Indian saris as a wedding gift.

Few Hollywood marriages have ended on such a genuine note of "no hard feelings" as that of Barbara Hutton and Cary Grant.

After Cary, Barbara's Hollywood interlude was over. For a while it looked serious between her and Freddie McEvoy, a notorious playboy-adventurer of the day, a "professional lover" and occasional dealer in the black market. His lust for the good things of life had made doormats of many people. He was a handsome, muscular man, and apparently Barbara fell for him. But in the words of Walter Winchell, "Freddie never made it as Mr. Barbara Hutton. He sure tried, though."

An intimate friend of Barbara's, Anya Sorine, has attempted to analyze the Barbara of those years and the way she thought of men: "She dreams a dream and makes herself the heroine. If she likes a man, at that moment he starts to be a hero. She sees only the qualities she wants to see. She is like an actress. Her life is a book. It is not real, but she lives it, and she lives and suffers as any heroine. And then the dream is over. The hero dies and it is over, and then he is just a friend."

Freddie was an unlikely hero figure. And there was someone else in the picture who would have been an obstacle toward McEvoy's marrying Barbara: his wife. "Freddie's so-called affair with Barbara doesn't mean a thing," stated Irene McEvoy, adding, "and between you and me, I don't give a damn."

Freddie, to save face, scoffed at reports he was going to marry Barbara. "How can I, even if I want to? I'm still married." And they had a young daughter.

It is ironic that McEvoy, so hot to marry Barbara, was the one who introduced her to the man who would be Barbara's next husband, Prince Igor Troubetzkoy.

McEvoy and Troubetzkoy were occasional roommates, and together with their pal Errol Flynn the two would weave in and out of the increasingly stormy life of Barbara Hutton.

Thirty-five-year-old Troubetzkoy had been involved in some of McEvoy's dealings in black-market francs, and Flynn later remembered him as the "bag man" in a transaction whereby Errol exchanged bags of dollars for bags of francs, in the dead of night, in a park in France.

But Troubetzkoy's aristocratic good looks, his charm, and most importantly his title were all impressive and authentic. Former bag man or not, Barbara wanted him. (The prince's parents were Prince Nicholas Troubetzkoy, a Czarist favorite, and the former Countess Catherine Moussine Pushkin. Igor's brother Youka had once been in the limelight, when he was in the United States, as a successful actor in silent films.)

Barbara would be Igor's first wife, and she moved swiftly. In Igor's words, "We had dinner, and—my God!—how fast!" (He later described Barbara as "an animal who is the product of America's development.")

Barbara's lifestyle and wealth astounded even Troubetzkoy. Igor's brother remarked, "All that money is very pleasant to think of, and is enough to give an ambitious young fellow buck fever when he sees the big opportunity. However, his mind is clear enough to reject the idea that money could be an obstacle."

The Prince subsequently muffed the "big opportunity." On the eve of their marriage, Barbara reportedly offered him one million dollars in cash, as a wedding present. He refused, as any "true gentleman" would. He would regret this gesture.

They were married in the fairytale setting of Chur, Switzerland, on March 1, 1947. Barbara was obviously in an excited state, because she signed the marriage registration "Barbara Troubetzkoy Grant."

Troubetzkoy would soon discover that life with Barbara wasn't a romantic paradise. At Barbara's request, they had separate bedrooms, a situation Troubetzkoy was unhappy with, but, "I said nothing to her about that." He saw and disapproved of how she literally starved herself to keep slim, but he was no more able to change her habits than previous husbands had been. Troubetzkoy was powerless to alleviate her insomnia or change her chain smoking. She was often remote and kept to herself for long periods. At times she would be gay and charming; at other times she would be silent for days on end.

Troubetzkoy later said, "I could see her today and know how she would feel tomorrow. But I was unable to help."

Regarding Barbara's lovemaking, one must read between the lines of Troubetzkoy's candid comments. "When everything is sustained by stimulants and emotions, then it is all right, but otherwise no." He added, "Every man knows only his own experience and what he feels. Perhaps another man would have a different story." He stated that their life together was "not a physical life. Barbara, you see, is in love with love."

By May 1947, six months before Barbara's thirty-fifth birthday, her health took a severe turn for the worse. Her starvation diets had done terrible damage, and she finally collapsed, victim of a serious kidney malfunction. She spent weeks being treated at the Salem Hospital in Switzerland. Her condition became critical, and she asked her doctor, Walter Hadorn, to send a telegram to none other than Baron Gottfried Von Cramm, imploring him to come to Barbara's side. One can imagine the humiliation Prince Troubetzkoy must have felt.

Von Cramm flew to Barbara and Barbara surrounded the handsome Baron with flowers, silk shirts, "presents from Cartier and money." With Von Cramm in attendance, "the poor little rich girl's" condition improved dramatically. Soon she was pronounced out of danger. Von Cramm accepted a grateful Barbara's parting gift of a new wardrobe, and returned to Germany. The Baron would visit Barbara, at her request, often over the next few years. Troubetzkoy, a sophisticated man, could only stand aside and be an "understanding mate."

Barbara was back in the hospital early in 1948, this time for surgery for an ovarian tumor. Barbara's hospital confinements were almost more harrowing for Prince Troubetzkoy than for Barbara, and probably out of desperation he became interested in the high-risk sport of auto racing. (The most dangerous sport he had participated in before this was bicycle racing.) Barbara bought him automobiles, but she disapproved of his participating in the sport.

When Barbara wasn't in hospitals, the Troubetzkoys lived mostly in hotels, a style of life the Prince abhorred. "Real luxury is to be in your own home, surrounded by beautiful things, by silence, by the quality of the people you have around, by the quality of their thoughts and feelings," he said. "This is something you cannot buy. That is something Barbara never had."

And never wanted, apparently. Barbara was spending what people who cared about her considered and unhealthy amount of time alone in bed, listening to music, writing poetry. According to Troubetzkoy, Barbara's conception of life was " 'Tomorrow, tomorrow, but not today.' She always anticipates tomorrow without knowing what she is searching for."

Troubetzkoy encouraged her to consult a psychiatrist, and she did, but nothing came of it.

Their entire marriage, as far as the prince was concerned, seemed a senseless, nonphysical, unhappy union. Barbara was "a lonely creature and when she is ill wants no one near her." Igor had given her a dog, which she adored—for a while. Then: "Take this thing away and give it back to Igor," she told her maid. Barbara was, in Igor's opinion, bored, bored, bored.

So Igor devoted his time and energy to auto racing. However, he had a bad accident and had to give it up. In a last-ditch attempt to start a new life with Barbara, he bought a magnificent small château (it had been converted from an old mill) outside Paris. Barbara paid for the house. The Duke and Duchess of Windsor were neighbors. The eighty-thousand-dollar fairyland retreat was a warm, wonderful home, but Barbara never saw it. She simply wasn't interested.

It was 1950, and Barbara had discovered a new playmate. He was another prince—Henri de la Tour d'Auvergne. The devastatingly charming young aristocrat loved to write poetry, and soon it was obvious that Barbara was in love again. She never went behind Igor's back with her new relationship. Quite the contrary—she let Troubetzkoy know whenever she was going on a weekend jaunt with Henri!

One of the *New York Daily News*'s foreign correspondents latched on to the story and cabled it to New York: CHANGING PRINCES? IT'S ALL NONSENSE TO BABS.

Soon afterward, Prince Troubetzkoy moved out, obviously furious because Barbara had humiliated him once too often. He engaged attorney Melvin Belli (who had been introduced to him by their mutual friend Errol Flynn) to handle the divorce. Belli contacted Barbara's representatives and demanded $750,000 as his client's divorce settlement. Graham Mattison replied that $500,000 was the limit. Belli relayed this information to Troubetzkoy, who, after deliberating the matter, decided they should take it.

Belli thought they shouldn't, but Mattison, totally familiar with the prince's background, countered that the half million was already "too much, and we will withdraw that offer if there is any dirty business." (The prince later stated that Mattison had always thought of him as a crook.)

Belli's reluctance to settle for less than the $750,000 was understandable. His fee was to be $100,000, plus disbursements, if he could get Prince Troubetzkoy that princely sum.

But Mattison called their bluff. Barbara was prepared for

a court battle and was furious that Troubetzkoy had placed her in such a predicament. Barbara was prepared for a fight, regardless of the bad publicity. She branded Troubetzkoy "the meanest man I ever knew."

Igor now had to resort to black market-like tactics. He couldn't prove in court that Barbara was philandering with Henri because he hadn't hired private detectives to follow them. But Igor was "resourceful" and, with his brother, "recovered" from Prince Henri's apartment some intimate letters Barbara had written to her new lover.

But Barbara didn't seem to care what people said or thought. She was throwing caution to the winds. One colorful incident, at the El Morocco in New York, never found its way into the news. It was deliberately withheld from the press because those managing the chic watering hole felt they would lose Barbara's patronage if it were printed that the Woolworth heiress, apparently drunk after consuming too much champagne, crawled under the piano and remained there, legs crossed, as the band played on.

A sad poem Barbara wrote during this period, which seemed to portray her state of mind, was printed by her friend Cobina Wright in Cobina's *Los Angeles Herald-Express* column:

> Nothing ever dies, neither day
>   nor pain,
> A flower is not born but to
>   blossom again.
> No anguish once known,
>   no rapture no need
> Lies barren and wasted for
>   want of a seed.

No darkness remains in the
  ultimate light,
Where shadows are suns at
  the closing of night;
And blessed is all that seemed
  ugly and sore—
Most beautiful this that was
  hurtful before!

Barbara tried for a quick Mexican divorce from Troubetzkoy, but her efforts backfired when Melvin Belli got wind of her intentions. Now Prince Troubetzkoy was forced to play his trump card. He had written a book, *My Life with Barbara Hutton,* and advised Graham Mattison he was planning to sell it. Mattison got the message, and by September 1951, a settlement was reached. It was nowhere near the five-hundred-thousand dollars Igor had been offered; it was around one thousand dollars a month for life, plus gifts from Barbara such as expensive automobiles, among other things. As for Barbara, it's interesting that in retrospect she considered Igor "the most understanding man in my life, the man who loved me most."

How did Troubetzkoy remember Barbara? "When someone talks about Barbara Hutton—my God, was I her husband? Is it possible I was married to her? I don't remember her physically. A man should remember a woman's body. But I don't remember!"

At one point in the film *Gone With the Wind,* when hordes of Northern soldiers are shown invading the South, the onslaught is described on screen by the title "Sherman." In the life of Barbara Hutton, the equivalent title would have to read, "Rubirosa," with a strong second billing going to Hungary's number-one export, Zsa Zsa Gabor.

Barbara was obviously desperately unhappy in the years immediately preceding her involvement with Rubirosa. She had said, "For a long time, I haven't loved. I really have nothing to live for. I decided if I was going to die, I wanted to die in Paris. I am just waiting to die." Rumors of suicide attempts had made the rounds, and both Prince Troubetzkoy and a well known Beverly Hills physician confirmed them.

But if Barbara had really wanted to die, she would have after the public ridicule and embarrassment she'd be subjected to as a result of her Rubirosa obsession.

Porfirio Rubirosa was the prime "catch," the most desired, glamorous stud in the international stable in the early 1950s. That in itself was reason enough for Barbara to want him. She had turned forty in November 1952 and seemed destined not to find whatever it was she was searching for. Perhaps the hotly pursued, gentle-voiced Rubirosa would be able to supply it—although how this could possibly be was anyone's guess, since Barbara's needs could hardly be fulfilled by Rubirosa's specialty. Physical lovemaking was not Barbara's requirement.

Rubirosa was to lovemaking what Tiffany has always been to diamonds, and his price was strictly in the Tiffany class. Barbara had met Rubirosa while he was still married to Doris Duke, who actually was—and still is—the richest woman in the world (her fortune is estimated at three hundred million dollars). Rubirosa had had to sign a marriage contract protecting Miss Duke's millions. But he received a one million dollar settlement from her.

According to Rubirosa, after he had been dating Barbara for a while, it was Barbara's idea to get married. "I did not want to get married. But she said, 'let's get married.' I said no, because I was afraid she would change. But she said, 'I promise not to change.' "

Barbara would be the fourth Mrs. Rubirosa. Wife number one had been Flor Trujillo, daughter of the dictator of the Dominican Republic. The marriage lasted five stormy years. Observers remarked this feat so impressed Dictator Trujillo that he appointed Rubirosa a diplomat.

Gorgeous French film star Danielle Darrieux was number two. Doris Duke had been number three. Rubirosa's expertise in the bedroom was legend in certain circles, complete with references to his prodigious natural equipment— eleven inches long and thick as a beer can. And he was an adept exploiter of those willing to purchase him.

Technically he was a career diplomat, working for the Dominican government. But he had been deposed as minister plenipotentiary to France from the Dominican Republic after he was named correspondent in a British divorce suit brought by golf star Robert Sweeney against his wife, Joanne, "the most beautiful debutante of the 1948 season." Then tobacco heir Richard J. Reynolds accused Rubirosa of breaking up *his* home.

But Rubirosa's adeptness at diplomacy—indeed, his genius for it—was evident when he remained in dictator Trujillo's good graces even after he had divorced Trujillo's daughter. Rubirosa was accurately pegged by society columnist Igor Cassini as the world's "Number One Foreign Co-respondent." He was also described as "the boudoir problem of the two continents."

This man was the prize Barbara was so eager to own.

At this time Barbara's major competition for Rubirosa's affections was not a sister multi-millionairess but a flamboyant, gorgeous woman whose appetite for publicity made even Barbara's penchant for headlines seem absolutely tame—the one and only Zsa Zsa Gabor.

Zsa Zsa, who received her first major press coverage when she was runner-up in the Miss Hungary contest in 1933, had accomplished the virtually impossible task of becoming a sex symbol after the age of thirty-five. In the youth-conscious United States this achievement has virtually remained unequaled, indeed unparalleled, and one can only be in awe of the woman's overwhelming drive and ambition.

Zsa Zsa had already been married three times. Her first husband had been a Turkish diplomat, Burhan Beige. Her wealthiest husband had been hotel magnate Conrad Hilton. (They had a daughter, Francesca, who, if Zsa Zsa is to be-lieved, has been fifteen years old for the past fourteen years. Apparently Francesca will remain a teenager as long as her mother is alive.)

At the time of the Rubirosa-Hutton "romance," Zsa Zsa, in her late thirties, was separated from her third husband, actor George Sanders, who had used Hilton's wedding ring when he married Zsa Zsa. Sanders was a notorious cheapskate.

While Zsa Zsa had been traveling in upper Hollywood circles for many years, her movie career had never really taken off. But she was a "colorful personality" and her career was moving in the right direction—until she entered the Rubirosa-Hutton arena.

"He is a passionate man and I know what I'm talking about," was merely one of dozens of provocative pearls to fall from Zsa Zsa's lacquered lips, and no one had any reason to doubt her. In retrospect she would enlarge on that evalua-tion: "He was the only man who really satisfied me in bed, because that was his profession: how to make love."

If lovemaking was his business, Rubirosa had plenty of satisfied customers. Barbara was one of the few who could pay his price, retail, and he would easily turn out to be the most traumatic purchase of her life. From this point on *P.R.* no longer meant *public relations* when discussing the life of Barbara Hutton—the initials stood for Porfirio Rubirosa.

Just before the "scandal," Zsa Zsa, together with her sisters Eva and Madga, had debuted their nightclub act at the Last Frontier Hotel in Las Vegas. The "gaudy Gabors," as some newspapers called them, were being paid twenty thousand dollars a week, and Zsa Zsa's show-stopping transparent gown had received publicity throughout the world. The costume, tasteless to some, fabulous to others, had obviously been "inspired" by Marlene Dietrich's see-through ensemble that had shocked and thrilled Las Vegas critics and audiences a couple of seasons earlier. Regarding big-bosomed Zsa Zsa's "plagiarism" of the costume, Marlene remarked, "I think audiences prefer quality to quantity, don't you?"

But Zsa Zsa was unstoppable. And although Rubirosa was indeed panting after her, he had told her that, for obvious reasons, he was going to marry Barbara Hutton. Zsa Zsa, the most sophisticated of Europeans, understood his thinking perfectly. She thought exactly the same way. "Rubi" loved *her*, but business was business, and marrying Barbara Hutton was big business.

Barbara's comment regarding all the advice she received not to marry Rubirosa: "In spite of what everyone says, I know I am going to be happy." Her decision to marry the Dominican playboy was, for her, pure pleasure, another indulgence she was permitting herself even in the face of certain disaster. The decision was hers alone. Her advisors, even Cary Grant and Baron Von Cramm, told her she was making a mistake. But Barbara had made up her mind, and at forty-one, she felt that her time to find Prince Charming was running out.

Incredibly, there had been no mention at all in the press of Barbara's intention to wed Rubirosa. The secret had been well kept. Then Zsa Zsa swung into action. ("Hell hath no fury like a Gabor scorned," subsequently scoffed reporters.)

She called a press conference, at which she wore a black eye patch and announced that Rubirosa's parting gift to her had been a punch in the face.

"Why?" asked reporters.

"Because I vouldn't marry him," replied Zsa Zsa.

She claimed that Rubi had said he would call off the Hutton marriage if only his beloved Hungarian would marry him.

"I tell him no," said Zsa Zsa. "I love George [Sanders], Rubi loves me, Barbara loves Rubi, but who loves Barbara?" she asked cattily, and then handled ensuing queries from reporters like Joe DiMaggio fielding fly balls—with grace and ease. Her flair for showmanship was formidable, and the news conference resulted in worldwide headlines making Barbara Hutton the sitting duck of the year for the tabloid press, which went to town.

The publicity snowballed. Television comedians wore black eye patches and launched into routines inspired by the unlikely new threesome—Babs, Zsa Zsa and Rubi. This had to be the most humiliating time of Barbara Hutton's life.

Time would prove that Zsa Zsa had cooked her own voluptuous goose insofar as her movie career was concerned. If she had been hoping the brouhaha would catapult her to superstardom, the effect was just the opposite. These were days before liberal attitudes about sex had saturated the nation. There was no swearing or nudity in "respectable" shows, in movies, or on television. Morality clauses were still very much standard in Hollywood contracts. For many public opinion makers of the day Zsa Zsa had, with her flaunting tactics, crossed the line of good taste. Louella Parsons would soon brand her behavior, in print, as "disgusting," and movie producers subsequently shied away from using her as though it had been revealed that she had starred in a porno film.

On December 30, 1953, Barbara Hutton married Porfirio

Rubirosa at the home of Doctor Joaquín Salazar, Dominican Consul in New York. After the register was signed Barbara asked Rubirosa, "Aren't you going to kiss me now? The press has waited so long."

The event was a circus. Lance Reventlow (now seventeen), Barbara's stepmother Irene and Jimmy Donahue were the only ones present who were related to the bride.

"I will make her happy at last," smiled Rubirosa.

"Oh, I would like to have another baby," said Barbara, "a child for my wonderful husband. But I am probably too old. I'm forty-one."

The new Mrs. Rubirosa, dressed in diamonds and a fashionable black ensemble, was a bundle of nerves. She was visibly shaking, and her eyes had a glazed look. (When Zsa Zsa was shown a picture of the wedding, she commented, "Barbara looks like she's on a death march. Maybe she should have worn white.")

"Maybe Zsa Zsa should have kept her mouth shut," wrote Walter Winchell, who despised Rubirosa.

Barbara would be quoted as saying, after the ceremony and reception, "I'm so tired I could die."

She looked it.

Zsa Zsa flew to New York and happily told reporters that Rubi was phoning her daily. She went to lunch and was photographed with ex-Hutton boyfriend Prince Henri de la tour d'Auvergne. In the words of many observers of the period, Zsa Zsa was behaving like "the first-class bitch of all time." To some she was, plain and simply, jealous.

For Barbara, things got worse so fast that her head must have been spinning. New York State officials questioned the legality of the marriage, since neither Barbara nor Rubirosa had had blood tests or obtained a marriage license. The Dominican government came to the rescue by claiming it hadn't been necessary, since Barbara was now a Dominican citizen, by special decree of President Trujillo. Furthermore, Trujillo reinstated Rubirosa as minister plenipotentiary to France from the Dominican Republic.

Zsa Zsa's story about Rubirosa's giving her a black eye took a back seat when it was revealed that he had given Barbara a broken ankle. Barbara lied to reporters and said she had slipped, but the truth was that Rubirosa had hit her so hard that she fell to the ground and broke her ankle. By Zsa Zsa's yardstick of love, did this mean that Rubirosa actually loved Barbara far more than Zsa Zsa?

It was too late for Barbara to back out now. The newly-weds flew to Palm Beach as scheduled, and Barbara had to be taken to the plane in a wheelchair. For their honeymoon she had rented the fabulous estate of the Maharanee of Baroda for ten thousand dollars a month.

At Palm Beach she confided to her old pal Cobina Wright about Rubirosa's actions and told her that Rubirosa "will kill me someday. I just know he will."

Jokes about Babs flooded the airwaves. "Spring must be here," quipped Bob Hope. "Barbara Hutton is doing her husband cleaning."

In the midst of all this, Rubirosa met Zsa Zsa on the sly, frequently in Phoenix, Arizona.

Meanwhile, Barbara bought Rubirosa his own plane, at a cost of two hundred thousand dollars. She also bought him an eight-hundred-thousand dollar citrus ranch (which would guarantee him a two-hundred-thousand dollar annual income.) This meant Barbara would have paid the same price for "Mr. Hung-like-a-horse" that Doris Duke paid. (It also proved Rubirosa's savvy as a businessman. The citrus ranch's value would increase, and it would always return a large income.)

Rubirosa could hardly be termed grateful. His first flight on his new plane was to New York for another rendezvous with Zsa Zsa. They made no pretense of keeping things secret. At one point it even seemed they might costar in a film, but the deal never went through.

Then, in a shockingly ungentlemanly gesture, he issued a statement about his marriage to Barbara: "I do not think Barbara is a sick girl, but for some reason she does not want to participate in an active life. She prefers to stay in bed all day. After seventy-three days of such an existence I knew that our marriage could not work out. I tried my best to stand it, but I knew if I left her I would be pronounced the villain and the betrayer of womanhood. At forty-five I am a healthy man. I am horrified at the thought of a healthy person who stays in bed all day, as Barbara did. I truly wish that my wife would abandon her way of life."

By April 1954, Rubirosa announced, "My marriage is finished, and I cannot be expected to stay home all by myself." He flew to meet Zsa Zsa. Barbara fled the country. Incredibly, she was already thinking ahead to a meeting with the man she had "really loved" and turned to these many years, Baron Von Cramm.

After Rubirosa, Barbara's psyche had to be in a bedraggled state. Without a Steve Hannagan to run interference for her with the press, her writeups had been disastrously unflattering. Her "ex-friend" Elsa Maxwell had written, "I suspect Barbara always will be resented in her own country as a spoiled snob who buys foreign gigolos. Barbara is condemned by her past record."

By mid-1955 she was free of Rubirosa, who never did marry the talkative Zsa Zsa. (He died in an auto accident a few years later. He was then a wealthy man, married to a young French woman.)

Barbara journeyed to her fabulous palace in Tangier. Von

Cramm was waiting for her, as arranged. They couldn't meet in the United States because he never dared apply for a visa —he feared it wouldn't be approved because he had served a prison term for homosexual acts.

As always, Von Cramm had a tonic effect on Barbara. She seemed in good spirits again. Her affair with the Baron had spanned twenty years, and Barbara was finally getting her way. "I should have married him eighteen years ago," she said. "So many things would have been different. But it was not possible, and even now it is a dream. He is the only one who has really wanted me to love him."

Barbara became Baroness Von Cramm on November 8, 1955. They were married outside Paris, and in perhaps a classic example of the old adage that people's characters never change, she expressed annoyance that there wasn't a crowd of spectators at the courthouse!

However, she had, in effect, jumped from the frying pan into the refrigerator. If Rubirosa had been a sexual virtuoso, a classically hot Latin lover, Von Cramm was as cool in the boudoir as a cake of ice.

The dream was kaput by the spring of 1956.

Blue blood Philip Van Rensselaer was many years younger than Barbara Hutton, but she never batted an eye at the age difference. She was in love again, thank God! Life to her without men was "worthless." Van Rensselaer's bank account didn't reflect his ancestry, but Barbara remedied that. Philip eventually admitted that Barbara gave him large sums of money. "She said I was a gentleman and I was meant to have lots of money. And anyway, she wasn't paying for me, Grandpa Woolworth was."

But in Van Rensselaer's opinion, "Barbara didn't know the right people from the wrong people." Echoing Cary Grant's opinions of a decade and a half earlier, Philip found many of her friends to be a largely "phony foreign entourage."

Some of these "friends" attempted to interest her in buying questionable works of art. "I tried to tell her, but she didn't even want to hear about it," said Van Renssaeler. "One day I begged her to get up—she had been in bed for two months!—and we went out. But she got sick and then we went home again. It was very boring, really. But I felt sorry for her."

Van Renssaelaer made the mistake of announcing that he and Barbara would be married. That permanently cooled Barbara on the relationship, and to Van Renssaelaer's dismay, she moved on.

She dated James Douglas, the twenty-seven-year-old son of the secretary of the air force. They were shopping in a San Francisco department store when a salesclerk recognized Barbara and said, "Miss Hutton, your son looks simply wonderful!"

"That's not my son," answered forty-seven-year-old Barbara in a huff. "That's my husband."

He wasn't, of course, and Barbara had no plans to elevate him to that lucrative estate.

Barbara's son was now making headlines on his own. He was a sports-car enthusiast and an expert at race driving, winning many competitions. In addition, "I guess you might say I'm a playboy," he cheerfully admitted to interviewers. He considered Cary Grant "my foster father," and Grant introduced him to many of Hollywood's most eligible beauties.

Lance soon showed signs of being a chip off the old Hutton block in more ways than one. In 1960, amidst much publicity, he married actress Jill St. John in San Francisco. Barbara was present but avoided the spotlight.

On a visit to Tangier, Barbara had met a "beautiful young

prince." He was an Indonesian, Raymond Doan, initially described as "an artist." He was Prince Doan Vinh Na Champacak, and in April 1964, six months before Barbara's fifty-second birthday, they were married in Mexico.

Prince Doan commented, "My wife is a Buddhist by instinct," a fascinating observation. The prince was Barbara's seventh husband.

That same year Lance Reventlow divorced Jill St. John and married nineteen-year-old former Walt Disney Mouseketeer Cheryl Holdridge. Barbara did not attend that wedding.

Poor Barbara was still being frequently hospitalized for "intestinal pain." Were her illnesses physchosomatic, and had they always been? She has never had an ailment that could remotely be characterized as "possibly fatal."

In 1966 Barbara suffered a devastating blow. She lost forever "the one man who can really make me laugh." Her beloved cousin Jimmy Donahue died, old and haggard at fifty-one. She was heartbroken by the loss.

Matters with Prince Doan went as they had with all her husbands and ended in the usual manner—a cash settlement. In this case there was an unusual twist. In addition to a check for three million dollars to Prince Doan, there was a check for one million dollars to his brother Prince Ronald. Why the brother received a million dollars remains a mystery.

In July 1972, Barbara received the greatest shock of her life. Lance, thirty-six years old, was killed in an airplane accident. He had been flying his own plane, a single-engine Cessna 206, which went down in the Colorado Rockies.

Barbara was now miserably, irrevocably alone.

The years have not been kind to the "Dollar Princess." She is almost never seen in public now and is apparently no longer ambulatory. When she does venture out, her chauffeur carries her to and from her automobile.

What has her life added up to? She has spent around thirty-five million dollars. But examining the countless photographs of Barbara Hutton that have appeared throughout the world over the past four and a half decades, tracing her life, one is struck by the jarring fact that in literally 95 percent of them, including those taken at her weddings, she is not smiling. She is always either gazing suspiciously at the camera or looking sullen, unhappy, or bored. That has been the story of her life.

Barbara Hutton isn't in *Who's Who*, the *Almanach de Gotha*, or the *Social Register*. But in the civilized world, there are few people over thirty-five who don't know who she is and that she's been here! Obviously, to have survived, she possesses more inner strength than most people—including perhaps herself—have given her credit for.

Another marriage? It seems totally unlikely, almost impossible. But in the words of society columnist Suzy: "I guess as long as Barbara is breathing, she's still eligible."

Barbara Sears Rockefeller
versus
Winthrop Rockefeller

A Supreme Court curtain, raised for a spicy pretrial examination of Winthrop Rockefeller in a suit brought by Joseph Sax, former attorney for Bobo Rockefeller, dropped with a bang on October 21, 1955, when Rockefeller's counsel refused to let him answer questions about intimate personal matters. Such matters included adultery and an extensive collection of pornographic material to which Bobo, his bride at the time, allegedly objected—also, too many whiskey bottles.

Pornographic material? Too many whiskey bottles? Adultery? A Rockefeller? The world would not have been more surprised than if President Eisenhower had been seen walking arm in arm with a notorious madam in a red-light district.

Winthrop Rockefeller, the grandson of the oil billionaire, married Barbara Sears, daughter of a Pennsylvania coal miner, on February 14, 1948. It was called "the Cinderella wedding of the century," and for Winthrop and Bobo, those were days of wine and roses.

But sparks were not long in flying. The flames finally flickered out eighteen months later, and they separated. Winthrop and Bobo, with love now turned to ashes, embarked upon years of well-publicized battling, and the period between the separation and the divorce was filled with acrimony, strife, and bitterness.

The idyll of Cinderella and Prince Charming was changed to the trials and tribulations of Beauty and the Beast.

Bobo Rockefeller was born Jievute Paulekiute in Oakdale, Pennsylvania, the heart of the coal fields. The year was 1917. At the age of two she went to live on her grandparents' small farm in Lithuania. She stayed there almost three years and returned to the United States speaking only Lithuanian.

Not long after Bobo's return her parents were divorced. Her mother, taking Bobo and her younger sister, Isabel, moved to Chicago and went to live with an aunt and uncle in a fourth-floor flat "back of the stockyards" on South Morgan Street. Mrs. Paulekiute then went to work as a seamstress in a mattress factory, and Bobo started elementary school four blocks from her home.

Life was far from easy for Bobo. At fourteen, now attending Englewood High School, she did baby-sitting and house cleaning, and gave dancing lessons to earn spending money. Since her ambition then was to become a ballet dancer, the dancing lessons served a double pupose—practice and income.

If life was far from easy, it also was far from dull. Bobo was the neighborhood tomboy and "good looker." She was by far the best female athlete around, and she played with both the girls' and the boys' baseball teams—the only girl so honored. As a swimmer she was easily one of the best, and as a dancer she was by almost unanimous acclaim "in a class by herself."

Bobo was almost a fictional picture—a very pretty, wholesome-looking all-American girl playing on the streets of the slums of Chicago, living proof that some people can flower and bloom in almost any soil.

In high school Bobo was very popular with her classmates and did well scholastically. In spite of the necessity of working at many odd jobs to earn money, Bobo found time, without too much training, to win the prestigious high-jump championship of the Chicago public-park system.

One of her classmates at Englewood was a good-looking, quiet, studious boy named Ralph Capone, Jr., whose uncle was quite well-known in Chicago and around the country. His name was Al Capone.

Then there was a very pretty girl, Marva Trotter, who would marry the heavyweight champion of the world, Joe Louis.

Later, when Bobo attained celebrity status, many of her classmates would point with a feeling of importance to having attended Englewood with her. In fact, so many claim to have gone to Englewood High with Bobo that it must have been the largest class in the history of education.

In 1931, her mother married Peter Necekas after a two-year romance, and the family moved to an eighty-acre farm in Lake County, Indiana, about five miles south of Lowell.

By the age of sixteen Bobo had developed into an out-and-out beauty. She was now known as Eva Paul, the *Paul* being a contraction of her father's last name, and Eva an anglicization of Jievute.

With her abundant good looks she was literally pushed into local beauty contests by doting friends and relatives, and she easily won them all. At these contests, her amazing resemblance to Ann Harding, then a reigning film favorite, caused quite a number of startled glances and double takes and numerous inquiries whether she was related to the star.

Looking for bigger worlds to conquer, Bobo won the title of Miss Lithuania at the Chicago World's Fair in 1933. Competing for the big prize, she was runner-up for the crown of Miss Universe, narrowly missing the title.

Miss Lithuania attended Northwestern University for a time and was very frank about her scholastic career. "I entered Northwestern in 1933. I didn't graduate, but I didn't flunk out either. I realized I wasn't too good a student and quit after about a year and a half."

After Northwestern, Bobo went on the stage—show business was a logical step to take. She had talent, beauty, and a drive to succeed. With that combination, and the "breaks," many have climbed to the top. Without the "breaks" many have not. However, as George M. Cohan often said, "The harder you work the luckier you get." One thing Bobo proposed to do, and did, was to work hard.

In 1938, after two years with stock companies, she appeared in the musical *Knights of Song*. Using the stage name Eva Paul, Bobo was playing the role of Pearl in the Boston company of *Tobacco Road* when she met Richard Sears, a Boston socialite, at a Christmas Eve party on Beacon Hill.

It was a whirlwind courtship, and they were married in Washington, D.C., on February 10, 1941. Actually, *this* should have been called Bobo's Cinderella wedding. Her subsequent Winthrop Rockefeller marriage was more of a Cinderella rerun.

The Sears family were top-drawer blue bloods, "proper Bostonians," who considered anyone who hadn't acquired great wealth and social position before 1850 as newcomers— and that included the Rockefellers. Bobo thus entered a family where the later marriage to Winthrop was considered almost a social backward step.

During her marriage to Sears Bobo met her large circle of

socialite friends. She glittered in her new surroundings, and her later marriage to Rockefeller did not much widen her social sphere, for she already knew almost everyone.

The "proper Bostonians" got along very well with Bobo, and she with them. Curiously, Bobo did not find them much dissimilar to her own family, except for their wealth. She said, "My mother was a strict, old-fashioned European. She wasn't too different from the correct Bostonians I hobnobbed with during my first marriage."

Bobo also got along extremely well with her in-laws, and it was her father-in-law who fondly gave her the nick-name "Bobo."

Ten months after the marriage, the country was in World War II, and Richard Sears, Jr., went into the navy. Bobo returned to her stage career. There was little else for her to do.

She filed an application in court to change her name from Eva Pauliski, also known as Jievute Paulekiute Sears, to Barbara Paul Sears. She explained that her family name was Pauliski, but her stage name was now Barbara Paul Sears. She had changed it from Eva Paul to Barbara Paul because there was another actress named Eva Paul, and it was causing confusion.

Using the name Barbara Paul Sears, Bobo performed in *You Can't Take It with You* with Fred Stone, appeared in several motion pictures, including a few Westerns, and played the lead in a picture directed by Walter Huston, who commended her talent highly. She seemed to be successfully climbing the slippery ladder to stardom.

After the war Richard Sears Jr., entered the diplomatic service and was appointed the second secretary in the American embassy in Paris. However, for Sears and Bobo apparently a diplomat's life and the stage did not make for a happy marriage.

Bobo met Winthrop Rockefeller in September 1946 in New York. They were introduced by Bobo's friend from the Sears social set, Mrs. John Hay Whitney, better known as Liz Whitney, the multimillionaire owner of some of the best thoroughbreds on the American turf, including a winner of the Kentucky Derby.

Winthrop recalled his first meeting with the future Mrs. Rockefeller: "I first met Bobo at a restaurant in New York City. My brother Laurence and I were having dinner together, and Liz Whitney came over and said, 'I have a perfectly charming girl I'd like you to meet, Winthrop.'

" 'Bring her along,' I said.

"She brought Bobo, and when I saw her I knew I was gone."

For Winthrop, "All those years of bachelorhood faded. All the other girls I had known faded, too. It was love at first sight. And remember, all this happened on what was in effect a blind date. Yes, sir, it took a blind date to get me married."

To his credit, Winthrop recognized a winner when he saw one. Bobo was unostentatiously charming, with a direct simplicity that no one could assume, as columnist Dorothy Kilgallen wrote, "unless it sprang from the heart."

"It was Bobo's utter candor, her naturalness, that makes her the one girl in the world for me," stated Winthrop. "And as you know, she is gloriously independent. When her husband went to work in the embassy in Paris and she was left alone, she didn't sit down and pine. She hitched up her belt and did something to keep her mind occupied. She had gone to dramatic school, and she took advantage of her training.

"I saw some of the pictures she played in, and believe me, she was good."

Events moved swiftly, and meeting friends for lunch in the Waldof-Astoria soon after meeting Bobo, Winthrop was in high spirits. "I've met the most beautiful girl in the world. With brains!"

After listening to Winthrop at that lunch, Woolworth Donahue, a close friend, said he could almost hear Mendelsohn's Wedding March playing for the country's most eligible bachelor. Woolworth said that somehow he knew "this was the real thing."

When Bobo met Rockefeller she was separated from Richard Sears and was living on the top floor of a four-story walk-up at 921 Third Avenue, between 55th and 56th Streets in Manhattan. The building was owned by the Sears family, and Bobo lived there rent free.

This was a slum area, with the Third Avenue Elevated trains roaring by night and day, but Barbara's apartment was far from a slum. In fact, it was magnificent. Although other tenants in the building had cold-water flats, the Sears place had its own heating plant and was completely redecorated when Bobo moved in. She shared the apartment with her sister Isabel, now a chemist working in Bound Brook, New Jersey.

The Rockefeller romance flowered, with the roar of the elevated trains a lullaby as Winthrop went courting. Walking up four flights of stairs did not put a damper on the romance. As Winthrop said, "I did not walk up. I floated."

On December 18, 1947, in Carson City, Nevada, Bobo obtained a divorce on the ground of mental cruelty. Two months later, on February 14, 1948, Barbara Paul Sears became Mrs. Winthrop Rockefeller.

They were married in the elaborate lake house at the Palm Beach estate of Winston Guest, America's premier polo player. It was a simple single-ring ceremony, in which Barbara was not asked to "obey" her strapping six-foot-three millionaire mate, although she had said earlier she was quite willing to do so. The word *obey* is no longer used in the Presbyterian marriage ceremony.

It seemed a prophetic omission.

A quiet, reserved Laurence Rockefeller, brother of Winthrop, served as best man, and a happy, bubbling Isabel Paul was the maid of honor.

The marriage was performed at 12:14 A.M. on Valentine's Day. The odd hour for the wedding—just after midnight—resulted from a seventy-two-hour waiting period required by Florida law after a license is obtained. The time is computed from midnight to midnight. Winthrop said, "We had to wait three days by law; otherwise we would have been married as soon as we got the license. Of that I can assure you. As you can see, we are getting married the first minute we legally can."

The minister, the Reverend Winslow S. Drummond, pastor of the Presbyterian church in West Palm Beach, who was to officiate, did not appear until midnight, and until his arrival nervousness was evidenced by some of the guests. "What happened?" wondered a few. "Are we going to have a cancellation? Will the golden coach turn into a pumpkin at midnight?"

The reason for the minister's lateness was right to the point: Since he could not legally perform the marriage until after midnight, he saw no reason to join the party until the ceremony could take place.

The ceremony was simple. The groom gave his bride a hearty kiss as soon as the final words were spoken, and a champagne toast was drunk to the newlyweds. Winthrop said exuberantly, "We'll be flying, but not by plane. It's great to be in love!"

The coal miner's daughter from Pennsylvania had traveled

an incredible path. Her first marriage had been to the social elite. Now it was to the richest bachelor in the country, and the blue-ribbon guests at the wedding included the most courted royal pair of the era, the Duke and Duchess of Windsor.

Bobo and the Duchess had much in common: both had risen from obscurity to the peak, although Bobo's beginnings had been considerably barer than Her Highness's. Only twelve years before the Duke had abdicated the throne of Great Britain for the twice-divorced American, "the woman I love."

Among the guests who weren't at the Rockefeller wedding, however, was Bobo's mother. Winthrop tried to get her to attend. He talked to her at length the day before and pleaded to let him fly her in. But she refused. She felt she would be out of place. She said diplomatically, "Thanks, but I just can't come. Papa and I have too much to do." Then she gave him some motherly advice. "Be good to Eva, Winthrop. If you're good to her she'll be good to you."

During the reception telegrams of congratulations began pouring in. One was from Bobo's father. Winthrop was not a snob. He seemed to take pride in the fact that Bobo's father was a coal miner, and he would have welcomed him to the ceremony. (A Pittsburgh newspaper had taken a picture of Paulekiute that morning at the coal mine, showing him in tears of joy at the pending wedding.)

Winthrop's father did not attend the ceremony either. If he shed tears, they were not of joy.

There was no telegram from Richard Sears. When informed of the nuptials he raised a diplomatic eyebrow and said, "Oh, is that so? Yes, you've got the record straight as to her being my former wife. I do not care to comment further."

Richard Sears's mother, who had a real affection for Bobo,

said, "She's a darling girl and delightfully pretty. But she and my son just didn't seem to get along together. I sincerely wish her the very best in her new marriage."

Photographers were allowed at the reception and had a field day. However, when Winthrop held up Barbara's left hand and lifted it to display a huge, rectangular stone that practically weighed down her hand, he said, smiling, "No pictures, please!"

It was an almost impossible request. It was like placing juicy steaks in front of starving men and saying, "Please don't eat them." After almost pathetic pleading by the photographers, Winthrop relented, and the world was able to see a diamond of startling size.

After ten days of short motor trips, sunning, swimming, and just relaxing, the happy couple went to live at Winthrop's sixteen-room triplex penthouse apartment at 770 Park Avenue, in New York City. A second residence for the newlyweds was a gabled house opposite Nelson Rockefeller's on the 3600 acre Rockefeller Pocantico Hills estate.

"I never saw people in the Rockefeller family work harder to make anyone feel at home," a friend of the family said, regarding the clan's attitude toward Bobo. "It just didn't work out. But they tried. They really tried."

On September 17, 1948, at the Polyclinic Hospital in Manhattan, a son was born. The premature baby was named Winthrop Paul Rockefeller.

One year later the Rockefellers were separated.

"The billionaire's son who married the coal miner's daughter," as newspapers now called Winthrop, was the fourth of John D. Rockefeller, Jr's, five sons.

Unlike his brother Nelson, who was elected to Phi Beta

Kappa at Dartmouth, or David, who was a Harvard graduate and had a doctorate in economics from the University of Chicago, Winthrop had little love of learning. In some of his courses he never opened a book, and he dropped out of Yale after three academically unspectacular years.

Winthrop was a nonconformist. After leaving Yale he went to work for Humble Oil as a roustabout in the Texas oil fields, where he dug pits and cleaned stills for seventy-five cents an hour. However, so hated was the Rockefeller name in the oil fields that Winthrop needed bodyguards for protection, although he was six feet three and weighed two hundred and fifty pounds.

In January 1941, pulling no strings and asking no favors, he joined the army as a private, and the following year he received a commission from officers' candidate school at Fort Benning. He was assigned to H Company of the 305th Infantry, 77th Division, and strictly on merit rose to the rank of major while fighting with the 77th Division in the invasions of Guam and Leyte. He was extremely popular with almost everyone with whom he came in contact in the army and was liked as a person, not as the scion of great wealth.

Enroute to Okinawa, Winthrop was wounded when a kamikaze plane struck his troop ship. Rockefeller's military career was over. He was discharged in 1946 as a lieutenant colonel, wearing a bronze star with an oak-leaf cluster and a purple heart.

After the war Winthrop, not surprisingly, joined the Socony-Vacuum Oil Company, at 26 Broadway, New York. It was not difficult for him to obtain employment there, since his family was a major stockholder. "With two hundred million dollars of his own, he doesn't really need the job," joked Socony executives.

Winthrop's wealth was a continuing topic of conversation, since a Rockefeller was working in a relatively minor job.

There was a straightfaced story making the rounds at Socony that Winthrop had *earned* his millions—he had expended hard work and diligent effort, and by the time he was two years old he was a multimillionaire.

Winthrop didn't exactly knock himself out at the office, and the nightclubs saw more of him than did the oil company. He seemed to go everywhere Broadway star Mary Martin went, and soon there was speculation that Mary's rendition of "My Heart Belongs to Daddy" meant Winthrop and wedding bells. For a while it looked that way.

However, it was soon an open secret that Winthrop's heart did not belong to any one woman but was apparently being shared by a dozen or more. And no one knew how many shared his pornographic collection, spoken of with awe and valued at more than one million dollars.

As one surprised reporter subsequently remarked, "I have a fifty dollar collection of French pictures, and I think they're pretty good. What does Winthrop have? A collection painted by Picasso?"

There was a good deal of discussion among Winthrop's friends about the porno collection. Did he use it to turn himself on, or to stimulate his female companions? As some of his friends said, "Winthrop didn't need anything to turn *him* on. He was always ready, willing and able."

The subject of Rockefeller's porno collection—in the years long before the public could pay to see "dirty" movies in dozens of theaters in the heart of Manhattan and throughout the country—was a wonderfully juicy topic for discussion.

At a distinguished gathering of the literati at the home of Dorothy Parker, Henry L. Mencken, nationally known author and stuffed-shirt deflater, was long and vehement in his defense of Winthrop and his personal rights. It was a dissertation few of his listeners, who included Associated Press feature writer Hal Boyle, forgot.

Mencken said, in his typical style, dipped in irony, humor, and seriousness, "It's really no one's business but Winthrop Rockefeller's if he wants to look at pornographic pictures. The Declaration of Independence gives every American the right to 'the pursuit of happiness.' And if looking at pornography helps Winthrop in chasing that elusive creature, I say, 'Go to it, Winthrop.' "

Mencken offered an amusing parallel: "Some people like to watch birds. That's not my cup of tea, and it may not be yours, but it's none of our business. What's wrong with watching birds if it makes a person happy? And if instead of birds Winthrop likes to look at pictures, what's wrong with that? There are some people who want to put clothes on animals!"

There was laughter and applause at this.

"If you go to the Metropolitan Museum of Art, to the Louvre, or to any of the great art centers of the world, you will see pictures that are pretty pornographic," noted a guest. "But it's called art. Many of Picasso's paintings, and some of Rodin's greatest sculptures, acknowledged masterpieces, are pure eroticism. Some are unbelievably erotic! Is that pornography? How can you make fish of one and fowl of the other? Furthermore, we don't notice too many of the ladies shielding their eyes when they look at sexy 'art.' They look. Believe me, they look!"

Mencken now jumped back into the fray. "I believe, so far as our outlook on the matter is concerned, that we could be guided by the motto of King Edward III when he founded the Order of the Garter, the highest and oldest order of knighthood in Great Britain.

"While King Edward was dancing with the gorgeous Countess of Salisbury at a court ball, she lost her garter. This, of course, was highly embarrassing to the countess, who was a close friend of His Majesty. 'Close friend' is what they called it in those days. As the king picked up the garter to hand to the countess, he saw several of his noble subjects smile and indulge in remarks. This made the king angry, and he decided that it would be a great, sought-after distinction to wear that garter. Sounds crazy, doesn't it? But that is how the highest and oldest order of knighthood was founded in Great Britain.

"The emblem of the Order is a dark blue garter, edged in gold, on which are printed the French words the king spoke as he handed the garter back to the Countess—'*Honi soit qui mal y pense.*' The translation bears repeating—'Shamed be he who evil thinks.' It is a matter of record that Edward's noble subjects saw the light and got the message fast. Maybe in this twentieth century we can learn something from that fourteenth-century king."

Mencken was now warming to his subject, and he continued, "Along this line, another Englishman, William Shakespeare, perhaps phrased it better than anyone when he said, 'There is nothing good or bad but thinking makes it so.'

"Perhaps some of the self-appointed caretakers of our morals may be interested to know that when we talk about the good old days of Victorian morality it makes one laugh to realize it is now becoming known that good old stern Queen Victoria, that paragon of morality, had an affair with her Scottish gardener that lasted for years. Queen Victoria! Sounds unbelievable? But it's true. His name was John Brown.

"And let me add that when it comes to what I may look at, I don't like the standards to be set for me by Emma and Ezra Jones of Hicksville Corners. They may like spinach and square dancing. I may like caviar and jitterbugging. A good rule is 'To each his own.'

"Again I say, 'Winthrop, if pornography makes you happy,

go to it. It's nobody's business but your own. Don't let Cactus Gulch tell you how to live.' "

Dorothy Parker later said, "I agree fully with Henry. What surprised me and a few of the others was the little tidbit about Victoria. Isn't that something? The only thing that would surprise people more would be to hear that Mae West is a virgin!"

After their separation Mrs. Rockefeller went to live with her mother and stepfather in Lowell, Indiana. For four years Winthrop took little interest in their son and continued to live a complete playboy life, engaged solely in the pursuit of pleasure. But in June 1953, he apparently underwent a change and made efforts to have Bobo agree to let him have custody of the boy.

This sudden paternal concern for his son did not sit well with Bobo. "My husband has always had visitation privileges. After all, we are neither legally separated nor divorced," she said. "Winthrop always has been welcome to see his child here in Lowell, but he has refused to come."

However, with the interest now shown by Winthrop in his son Bobo had hopes that a possible reconciliation might be effected. As she put it, "It would be for our son's sake, not for mine."

She was eager for an end to the hostilities, but not if it meant going back to the Rockefeller way of life. Her experience with *young* society at its top level was a sore disillusionment, and she had no great esteem for her contemporaries in the social set. The young women, she said vehemently, "cheat, drink, and lie."

Bobo retained an attorney, Joseph Sax, to negotiate a possible reconciliation.

After Sax consulted with Winthrop's attorney about the

possibilities, it was decided that Mrs. Rockefeller would reserve a suite in a Chicago hotel so that a meeting could be held to explore the matter on neutral ground.

The meeting was held, but it turned out to be far from a peace conference. Bobo later said, "It was a worthless meeting. They had no intention of a reconciliation. In fact, they all got together and said, 'You must have a divorce.'

"I said, 'I have no intention of giving him a divorce until he supports my child and me. There has been no support whatsoever for my child and myself for a full year. I did not receive a nickel from Winthrop. All I wanted was money for room and board. I just wanted not to have to ask my mother every day for two or three dollars for a dentist bill or for something else.

"I told Winthrop it was unbecoming for a Rockefeller not to support his wife and child, and the child should have the advantages of other children. I brought up the subject about a horse at the time and told him that my stepfather was buying a horse for Winnie.

"I said I thought it would be nice if his father had done that. I also asked Winthrop where did he want his child educated, but he was indifferent to it."

The get-together became bitter. Bobo continued, "Winthrop refused to give any money to me and Winnie at the meeting. I said, 'Very well then, will you please leave. I paid for these rooms at the hotel, which I can't afford. I borrowed to do it, and the next time you wish to discuss anything at all, you must come out to Lowell, Indiana. Will you please get out of this room."

According to Joseph Sax, what took place at the meeting was quite a bit different. It bordered on the frenetic. "There was a discussion of a possible divorce, to which Mrs. Rockefeller took violent objection. A little while later she said to

Winthrop, 'I hired this suite and brought you here. I need some money now. Give me two hundred dollars.' Mr. Rockefeller said, 'I haven't got two hundred dollars with me.' She said, 'Well, then give me a check for two hundred dollars.' Rockefeller said, 'I don't have a check.'

"With that, Mrs. Rockefeller stood up, walked over, took a punch at him, and screamed, 'Spend it on your tarts.' When she did that Mr. Pfeiffer [Timothy N. Pfeiffer, of Milbank, Tweed, Hope & Hadley] stepped in to interfere, and she took a slug at him. I stepped in and broke them up. As soon as I separated them Mr. Pfeiffer ran out of the door and was down the hall. I then separated Mrs. Rockefeller and Winthrop. She had him by the tie. I got her hand off the tie and pushed her over to a settee and sat her down, and with that Mr. Rockefeller ran out of the room."

Bobo's actions were no great surprise to her friends. She always stood up and was willing to fight for what she thought were her rights and never allowed *anyone* to walk over her.

The battle in the press now began. Winthrop claimed he had been refused permission to see his son. Through his attorneys he announced that a one million dollar trust fund had been set up for the benefit of his estranged wife, and he added that he hoped she would now be willing to let him have custody of their son at regular intervals.

Bobo's reply was swift and angry. "His concern for the boy is very touching. He never took any interest in him and has seen him only once since he was in diapers. He is now almost five years old. I have begged, pleaded, sent telegrams, called on the phone, put the child on the phone, and asked him to see the boy. I have offered to go to New York and offered to send my mother with the child to New York. He has refused. I even offered to take the child to Florida. The boy is not a can of oil, to be shipped all over the country." She added emotionally that she would be willing to take the youngster to New York to live, if her husband provided them with a home.

The sudden flurry of activity on Winthrop's part seemed to be tied to an intention to end the marriage finally and officially. Some weeks previously he had taken up residence in Little Rock, Arkansas, to meet the residency requirements of that state for a divorce. Under Arkansas law in 1953 a resident was permitted to start proceedings on the basis of a three-year separation.

Anxious to have the matter completed, so that he could proceed with a divorce, Rockefeller began negotiations on the amount he would give Bobo. On October 1, 1953, a dollar figure was apparently arrived at. Bobo was to receive, for herself and her son, $5.5 million, plus $70,000 in additional annual income.

The proposed settlement also provided that the son be provided with a separate trust of $1.5 million and that the boy's rights would be preserved as "an ultimate beneficiary in substantial trusts established by his grandfather." Bobo was to receive $2 million in cash as part of the $5.5-million settlement.

Bobo's lawyer recommended that she accept the offer. Bobo rejected it. She also changed lawyers. A fighting Bobo claimed, as she changed lawyers, that the much-touted settlement offered her was largely hot air, full of loopholes, and that she and her estranged mate were as far from agreement as ever.

During the time of the negotiations Bobo and her son had been living at Winthrop's triplex penthouse apartment. Winthrop had not invited Bobo to move in—Bobo had just walked in and seized possession, secure in the knowledge that a Rockefeller would hardly throw his wife and son out on Park Avenue.

Young Winthrop, five years old, found living in an apartment vastly different from the bucolic setting of life at his grandmother's eighty-acre farm in Indiana.

He liked romping through the rooms, and his favorite game was dialing Information and telling the operator he wanted to talk to the police department. At such times Bobo would speak sharply to him in Lithuanian, which he understood as well as he did English.

In spite of scoldings, Winnie enjoyed answering the phone. Once, when Bobo was out of the room for a minute, the telephone rang and young Winthrop answered it. When Bobo returned he said, "Someone called. It sounded like your lawyer, Mr. Nizer. So I told him you weren't home."

One summer's night, however, Winnie's escapades luckily avoided ending in tragedy because of a quick-witted maid. Winnie, used to life at the Lowell farm, where he would sometimes sit in a window with his feet dangling, saw no reason why he could not do the same in the Rockefeller apartment. The night was hot, and the time seemed appropriate. The fact that it was sixteen floors up did not seem to make much difference to the boy. The maid almost had a heart attack when she saw him with his legs outside the window. Luckily, she did not scream, and quickly pulled him in.

After everyone had taken tranquilizers, it was impressed upon young Winthrop that windows in a sixteenth-floor apartment were not quite the same as those in a farmhouse.

Bobo led a comparatively quiet life at the penthouse. She rarely dined out, and a thyroid condition following the birth of her son had given her an allergy to alcohol. Except for shopping in the department stores and seeing her lawyers, she seldom left the apartment.

From the day Bobo rejected the $5.5-million offer, she said she had not received one dime from Winthrop. She was in the peculiar situation of living in a swanky Park Avenue triplex without any money. Rockefeller was not paying any of the bills.

Needing a new vacuum cleaner, Bobo telephoned Winthrop's New York lawyers for permission to buy one. They authorized the purchase providing it did not exceed a hundred dollars. On receipt of the bill from the Madison Appliance Company, Bobo sent it to Winthrop for payment. His Arkansas attorney, Edwin Dunaway, sent it back to Bobo, saying that inasmuch as Rockefeller hadn't been consulted about it, "he feels it is Mrs. Rockefeller's responsibility."

The appliance company, finally tiring of waiting for payment, threatened to repossess the cleaner. Bobo had to borrow to pay for it. "I frequently had to borrow," Bobo said. "Every month I have to ask myself, 'What can I pawn?' "

To add to the confusion and aggravate the situation, Winthrop sold one of the three floors of the triplex, making it a duplex. "I'm supposed to take a hint," said Bobo. "They don't want me to live here. But I'm not getting out."

Bobo called a press conference to broadcast her plight. Instead of a conference she found herself playing a tearful leading role in a drama that could have been called "Locked Out."

When reporters and cameramen descended on 770 Park Avenue for the conference, the doorman refused to open the door, but instead opened a panel in the building's glass-and-iron-grilled front door. Bobo, her eyes red from weeping, peered out.

"I'm sorry—I'm locked in and you're locked out."

"On whose orders?" a reported asked.

"I don't know. I don't know why I am not allowed to

receive my guests. I want my guests in here, and I'm going to find out the reason I can't," said Bobo.

The doorman, who had opened the panel, then closed it. Apparently he had his orders, and they could have come only from the owner of the duplex-triplex, Winthrop Rockefeller. (The manager of the house said the door was locked and all persons entering were being screened because the tenants complained of the "tumult" caused by the Bobo-Winthrop controversy.)

As the reporters were leaving, one of Bobo's lawyers, Ephraim London, came out of the building, where apparently he had been conferring with her. He told the reporters, standing around on the sidewalk in front of the building, that he was Bobo's "personal lawyer." He emphasized that point, stating that Leo G. Fennelly was now her lawyer in "the matrimonial matter," having replaced Louis Nizer.

He said, "Mrs. Rockefeller is genuinely embarrassed by the action of the apartment-house manager in locking out reporters," and he shepherded the newsmen to the corner (73rd Street and Park Avenue) for an outdoor conference on a cold, blustery winter day.

He vigorously denied the statement of Winthrop's attorney that Bobo had set a figure of ten million dollars as a settlement. "At no time has Mrs. Rockefeller refused the offer made by her husband on August 29. She twice accepted the terms in principle. She had only raised some objections to some of the details which she felt had strings attached to them.

"She never questioned the overall amount but did raise some points on the various trusts."

London then read a statement, which he said Bobo had intended to give reporters at the interview.

" 'I have read reports that my husband claims he has not

been permitted to see our son except in my presence. My presence apparently places a constraint on my husband. I would like to repeat that my husband is free to visit our son alone any time he wants to. I shall be present only to introduce them.' "

Asked how recently Winthrop had seen his son, London replied, "Oh, he hasn't seen him in many years, not since he was a baby. And he hasn't tried to, as far as I know."

Bobo resented the statement that she was demanding ten million dollars, because of its implication that she was a gold digger. The radio and TV jokes that "Winthrop may remarry Bobo for *his* money" made her especially unhappy because she said she was actually down to her last few dollars.

Winthrop Rockefeller's reply was angry and sharp. Through his attorney he announced that Bobo had repudiated the $5.5-million settlement and was now demanding $10 million. "There is no apparent way of meeting Mrs. Rockefeller's insatiable financial demands," declared the attorney in a statement issued from Little Rock. "Furthermore, Mrs. Rockefeller has persistently made false and irresponsible public statements about the financial support she has received during their separation.

"She has accepted the income from the $1-million trust fund set up for her personal benefit, as evidenced by canceled checks despite her statements to the contrary. Although she has received $32,750 in 1953, on which she had to pay neither state nor federal income taxes, and a rent-free apartment, Mrs. Rockefeller has represented herself as being without funds on which to live.

"Mr. Rockefeller has been permitted to see their son only in the presence of Mrs. Rockefeller. On such occasions the boy has been subjected to an atmosphere of bitter and intense recrimination which Mr. Rockefeller is determined to avoid in the future because of the detrimental effect on their son."

This was a picture quite different from the one Bobo painted. The stories were becoming conflicting and confusing, and the name of the game seemed to be, "Whom are you going to believe?"

The talk around town was that the reason for the delaying tactics was that Bobo could not bring herself to face up to the fact that with a divorce she no longer would be Mrs. Winthrop Rockefeller.

It was reminiscent of Mrs. William Randolph Hearst's reluctance to divorce her husband so he could marry Marion Davies. Hearst was supposedly willing to pay thirty million dollars in cash in exchange for his freedom. Mrs. Hearst's lawyers advised against it. "Why should you accept? You would no longer be Mrs. William Randolph Hearst, and *that* is worth much more than thirty million dollars."

Hearst never got his divorce. But Bobo Rockefeller was not in quite the same financial boat as Mrs. Hearst, who was a multimillionairess in her own right, in a position to refuse the Hearst millions.

Bobo had felt that Louis Nizer was the perfect lawyer right up to the severance of their relationship. He had done a superb job representing Eleanor Holm Rose in her divorce from megalomaniacal Billy Rose—"The War of the Roses," the press had termed it—and Bobo had complete confidence that Nizer could effect as satisfactory a conclusion for her.

On August 20, 1953, Louis Nizer had written the Rockefeller attorneys that he was authorized to accept five million dollars for Mrs. Rockefeller and an equal amount for her son, plus a number of fringe benefits.

On August 28, Rockefeller rejected the demand and submitted a counterproposal, totaling $5.5 million, plus $3 million that Winthrop pledged to bequeath to his son. On October 1, there was an exchange of letters, and Bobo accepted the counteroffer of August 28, and requested additional benefits, to which Rockefeller agreed.

A short while later Nizer notified Winthrop's attorneys that he was drawing up the necessary papers. Rockefeller's lawyers never received them, because Bobo would not sign the agreements Nizer had drawn.

When Bobo balked at signing, Nizer threatened to withdraw as her attorney. With regret she accepted the fact that Nizer would no longer be her attorney. But she was worried there were possible loopholes in the agreement, and she would not sign.

Bobo substituted Leo G. Fennelly, of Fennelly, Eiger, Nager & Lane, of 48 Wall Street, as her attorney.

On December 30, Fennelly contacted Winthrop's lawyers and renewed Bobo's demand for ten million dollars. On January 4, 1954, Milbank, Tweed, Hope & Hadley advised Fennelly that Winthrop would not give Bobo one cent beyond the August 28 offer, which they claimed she had accepted.

To end the confusion and Bobo's claims of poverty, Rockefeller decided to deliver an ultimatum, calling on his wife to accept in writing, no later than January 8, 1954, the $5.5 million offered. Otherwise negotiations would be broken off.

Apparently the ploy was successful, for on January 9 a Rockefeller lawyer announced that "Mr. Rockefeller has instructed me to state that he is pleased that the agreement is no longer repudiated and that Mrs. Rockefeller has again decided to accept it."

The word "again" caused comment, for inferentially it had been accepted before. Why would acceptance now be more lasting? Bobo had previously stated that Rockefeller's offer was full of loopholes and that he could cut off her aid when he wanted. Had the loopholes been closed?

Before tackling any new endeavors, Winthrop was anxious to wind up his marital affairs. The Bobo outbursts and claims of being "hobo poor," so that she had to live off the charity of friends, was becoming embarrassing. To put a halt to it he had decided on the ultimatum, which had apparently proved effective.

Winthrop had originally gone to Arkansas to establish residence for a divorce, but it didn't work out that way, for it was Bobo who obtained the divorce in Reno, Nevada, on August 3, 1954. The ultimatum, and the attorney's announcement that it had been accepted, were not quite accurate. The final figure was $6,393,000—by far the largest matrimonial settlement ever made.

Although the divorce ended the marriage, other chickens of the lengthy squabbling were coming home to roost. Legal actions stemming from the attempt at reconciliation, but coming after the divorce, were to provide the most embarrassing revelations yet about Winthrop Rockefeller.

While awaiting the outcome of his marital difficulties, Winthrop began building an empire on a mountaintop in Arkansas. In 1953, while establishing a residence to meet the requirements for a divorce, he had purchased an initial tract of 927 acres of almost impenetrable forest for Winrock Farms atop remote Petit Jean Mountain, sixty miles northwest of Little Rock.

With a great deal of time and effort, and millions of dollars, the ranch eventually grew to about fifty thousand acres, on which he raised Santa Gertrudis cattle, acquired from the King Ranch in Texas. He paid $31,500 for his first Santa Gertrudis bull.

Winthrop's ambition was to enter politics, although a Republican running for office in Arkansas then had almost a zero chance of winning. In 1954 practically all officeholders were Democrats, and the Republican party was practically nonexistent in the state. Furthermore, Senator Joseph McCarthy and McCarthyism were hurting Republicans badly all over the country.

The beginning of the end of the rabble-rousing McCarthy as a power in politics were the nationally televised hearings of alleged widespread Communism in the army. The backlash was devastating to McCarthy and his witchhunts. In an effort to gloss over McCarthyism, President Eisenhower quipped that "McCarthyism is now McCarthywasm." But it wasn't quite that simple. The McCarthy brush had tarred the Republican party.

However, McCarthy was almost completely finished as a political figure when the United States Senate voted, by the overwhelming margin of 67-22, to censure him.

(John F. Kennedy, then a senator from Massachusetts, and his father, Joseph P. Kennedy, were very close friends of McCarthy's, and Robert Kennedy was a member of the senator's staff. Senator Kennedy did not vote on the censure and never spoke out against McCarthy.)

The McCarthy era seemed a bad time to enter politics in Arkansas as a Republican. In fact, it seemed hopeless. However, the tremendous infusion of Rockefeller dollars again proved that money is the mother's milk of politics and can work wonders.

Winthrop sent paid agents into every county in the state to set up party organizations. Money was literally poured like water into the arid Republican desert, and the party bloomed. Rockefeller was twice elected governor of the state, and he was the dominant figure in Arkansas politics for a decade.

It was not the first time in American history that great wealth had purchased high office.

There is little doubt that it was by the grace of Rockefeller money that Winthrop was elected governor; nevertheless, there is also little doubt that he did a great deal for the state. His successful efforts to induce business and industry to come into the state, his work in scientific farming and cattle raising, which made Winrock a scientific agricultural showplace, visited by farm experts from all over the world, and his attempts to make the government of Arkansas the active agent of social betterment earned him seven well-deserved honorary doctorates from leading universities.

It is ironic that Rockefeller, who did not graduate from Yale and never received a bachelor's degree, was entitled to be addressed as Doctor.

Winthrop Rockefeller had done so much for Arkansas that his heavy drinking habits, although widely known, did not prevent his election and reelection as Governor. It was no secret that on more than one occasion he addressed the legislature in a far from sober condition, but since many of the legislators were in the same shape there wasn't much finger pointing from that direction.

If heavy drinking and drunkenness were a bar to holding public office, quite a number of senators and congresspeople would be looking for other jobs.

After the divorce and settlement, Winthrop and Bobo were sued for legal fees by Joseph Sax, who had acted as attorney for Mrs. Rockefeller for a brief time. During an examination before trial, Sax's attorney opened a Pandora's box when he asked some highly embarrassing questions of Mr. Rockefeller.

What had been heatedly discussed in private circles was now about to burst forth for public consumption. "Did you in 1948 have an extensive collection of pornographic materials to which your wife raised objections?" asked Sax's attorney.

Winthrop could have said no and ended the matter, had that been the truth. But he didn't. Instead, Winthrop's attorney objected and said, ". . . I don't think we should go into all that dirty linen."

Another question along the same line could also have been answered by a simple *no* if that had been the fact. "Is it not true that your wife, during the time of your marriage, *repeatedly* objected to lewd and pornographic material which you kept in your home?"

The questions were dynamite laden, and Rockefeller's lawyer nicely solved the problem by stating, "We will not answer those questions. We will plead constitutional immunity."

"You mean you are going to plead incrimination," snapped Sax's attorney.

The objections to this line of questions were now numerous, and finally the attorney said, "Mr. Sax will eventually have to prove here what the subjects were upon which Mrs. Rockefeller engaged him. I am going to prove that the subjects were adultery, possession of pornographic materials, excessive drinking, consorting continuously with notorious women, and half a dozen other matters."

In reply to Rockefeller's contention that Sax was "going into a lot of murky business," Sax's attorney retorted that "the only things Mrs. Rockefeller talked to him about were the mud and the dirt."

One of the women with whom Rockefeller was alleged to have had sexual relations, both before and after his marriage to Bobo, was Virginia Sommers, a dazzling brunette nightclub singer, whom Winthrop had met on his nightclub rounds.

Several years before, Sax had sued Miss Sommers and

Rockefeller, among others, alleging that they had frozen him out of a television deal he had originated. To add to the bizarreness, Sax was also suing Miss Sommers for fourteen thousand dollars he had paid her because of a paternity claim against him. Sax claimed he had learned that he was not responsible for the pregnancy, "if indeed she was pregnant."

As a reporter present remarked with a laugh, "It looks as if you can't tell the players without a score card. Miss Sommers must have been one busy little singer. Singing lullabies. Maybe *she* was the reason Rockefeller moved to Arkansas!"

During the seemingly endless legal proceedings over the years, Bobo had, in one phase of the litigation or another, retained more than twenty lawyers. She may not have graduated from Northwestern, but she rivaled many of her attorneys when it came to knowledge of certain aspects of the law. She read law books on her own, and her lawyers were astonished at the extent of her knowledge of trusts, taxes, and out-of-state divorces.

One lawyer observed with admiration, "She talked to me for two days and really picked my brains. Then in the end, she didn't retain me. Know why? Because she didn't think I had enough men on my team! Winthrop, she told me, had three law firms, and his family commanded the services of specialists in everything from trusts to torts.

"I said that my associates and I were completely competent to handle the litigation, but she wouldn't believe it. After two days of listening to all I could tell her, she up and walked out. And I can name you quite a few other lawyers who had the same experience."

Bobo's explanation was, "I'm looking for the right lawyer, because I've found out you can't scare the Rockefellers." She would have had every right to add, "And the Rockefellers can't scare me."

Winthrop Rockefeller died at the Desert Hospital in Palm Springs, California, on February 22, 1973. He was sixty years old, young for a Rockefeller whose father lived to be almost ninety and whose grandfather and great grandfather to almost a hundred.

Millions of Winthrop's money and thousands of days in work had been used to create Winrock. When asked how he had found time for his ranch showplace, politics, and a far-from-neglected personal life, Winthrop answered, "It isn't the hours you put in that counts. It's what you put into the hours."

Winthrop, Jr., had attended the Rockefeller family-supported Browning School in New York and then the Le Rosey School in Switzerland, which has among its graduates practically all the nobility and the wealthiest families of Europe and the Middle East.

After Le Rosey he attended Oxford for a year. While at Oxford he met and married Deborah Cluett Sage, an heiress to the Cluett Peabody millions, who was attending the Queens-Gate School in London.

After his marriage, and while his father was alive, young Winthrop made his home at Winrock. Seemingly in furtherance of the wishes of the elder Rockefeller he attended Texas Christian University's ranch- management school, graduating in 1974, a year after his father died.

At his father's death the executors of the estate stated that Rockefeller had requested that if his son demonstrated a talent and commitment to the furtherance of Winthrop, Sr.'s plans for Winrock Farms, he be given preference when the property was sold.

In October 1975, the executors, having decided that the son had met the requirements and demonstrated "his talent and commitment to the furtherance of Winthrop Rockefeller's plans for Winrock Farms," sold Winrock to Winthrop, Jr., for $8,162,700.

This apparently is what Winthrop, Sr. had hoped would happen.

When all was said and done, none of the Rockefellers could claim that Winthrop had made a mistake in 1948 by marrying the coal miner's daughter from Pennsylvania. She had done a remarkable job in the turbulent and custom-shattering 1960s in raising their son to assume a place on the rarefied Rockefeller plateau.

Upon the death of his father, Winthrop, Jr., acquired more than Winrock. He became heir to his father's trusts, and as the only child of one of the five Rockefeller brothers he has become the wealthiest of the fourth generation of Rockefellers. Thus a coal miner's grandson takes his place among the monetary elite of the nation, with all the power that great wealth brings.

Millions of words had been written about Cinderella in the hectic days when Bobo was a household name and "life with Winthrop" was a conversation piece. But seldom is the name seen in print any more.

Bobo maintains apartments in New York City and Paris and keeps almost completely out of the public eye. She has never remarried, and when she writes her name, it is boldly signed, "Barbara Rockefeller."

After all, that *is* her name.